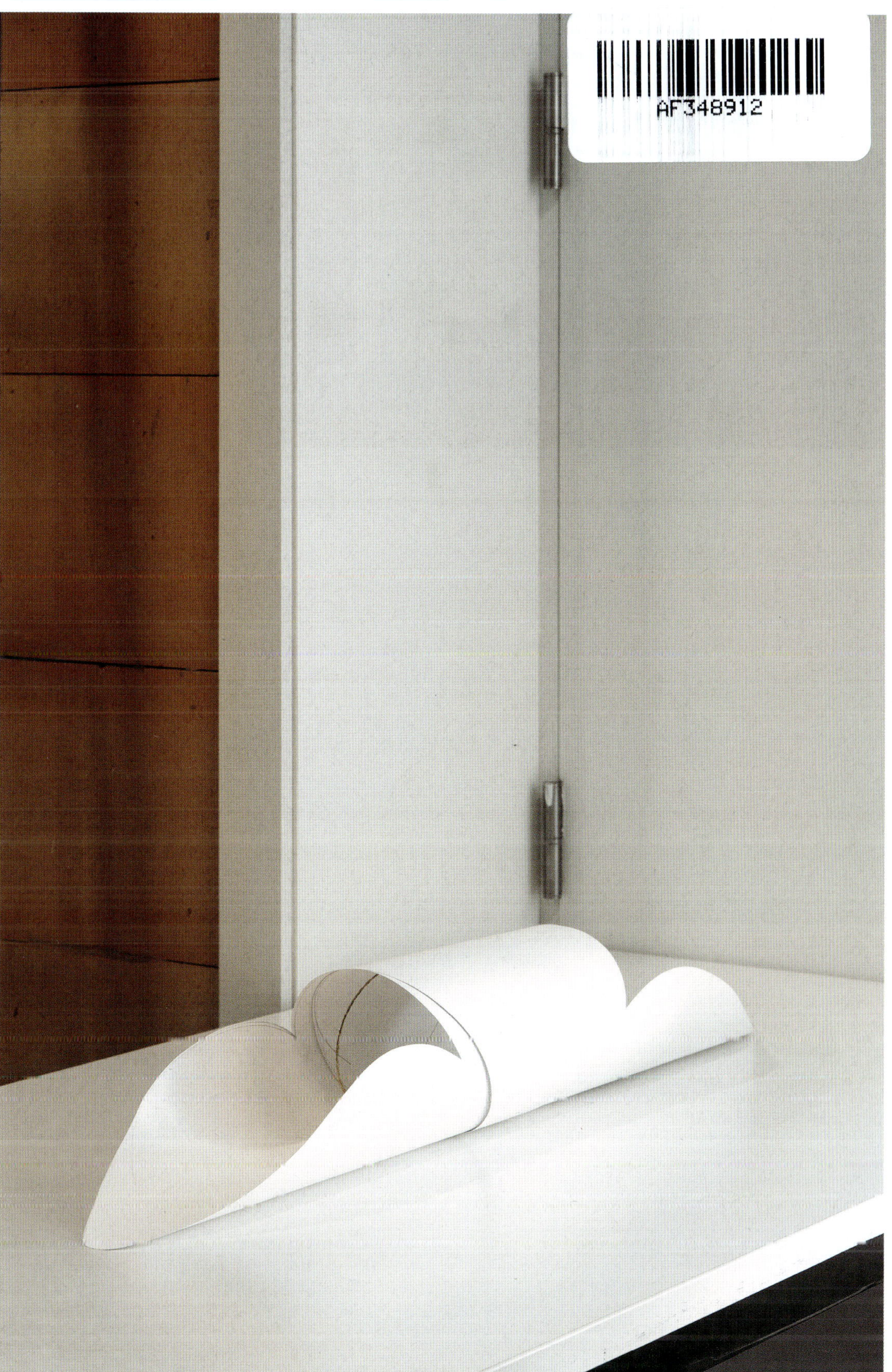

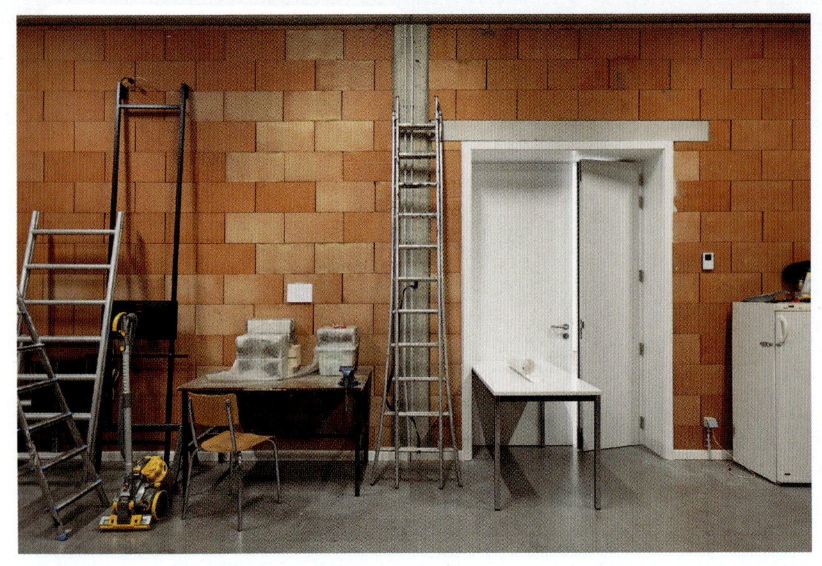

(24) Aaron Amar Bhamra & Céline Mathieu, *former tulip and string*, 2025, paper and pencil, string and metal wire, various dimensions, 5 + 2 AP
(2, 13, 3, 17, 16) *Fugue*, installation views, 2025

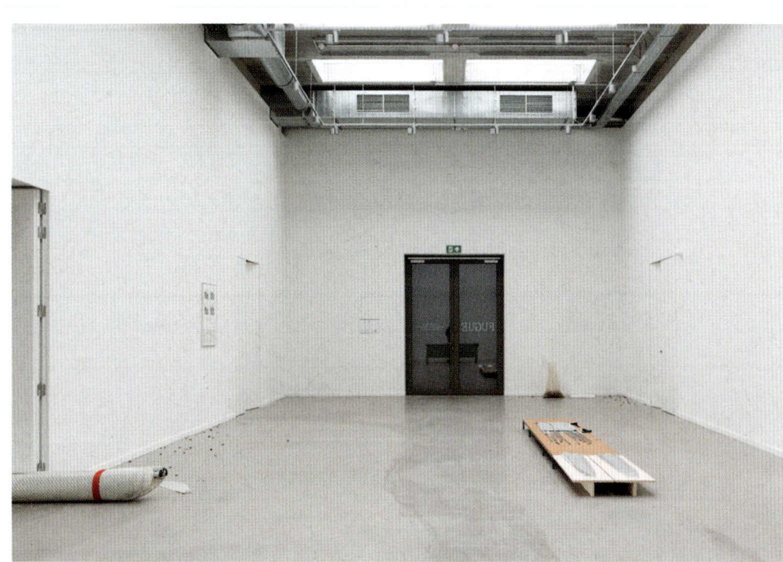

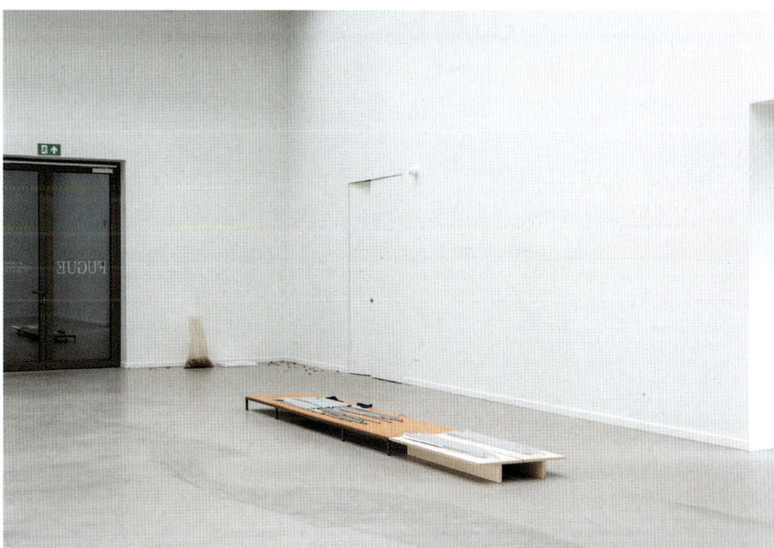

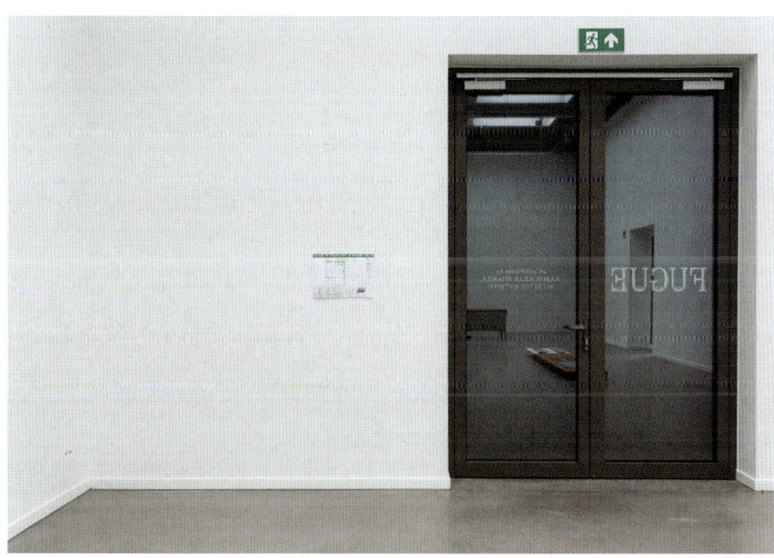

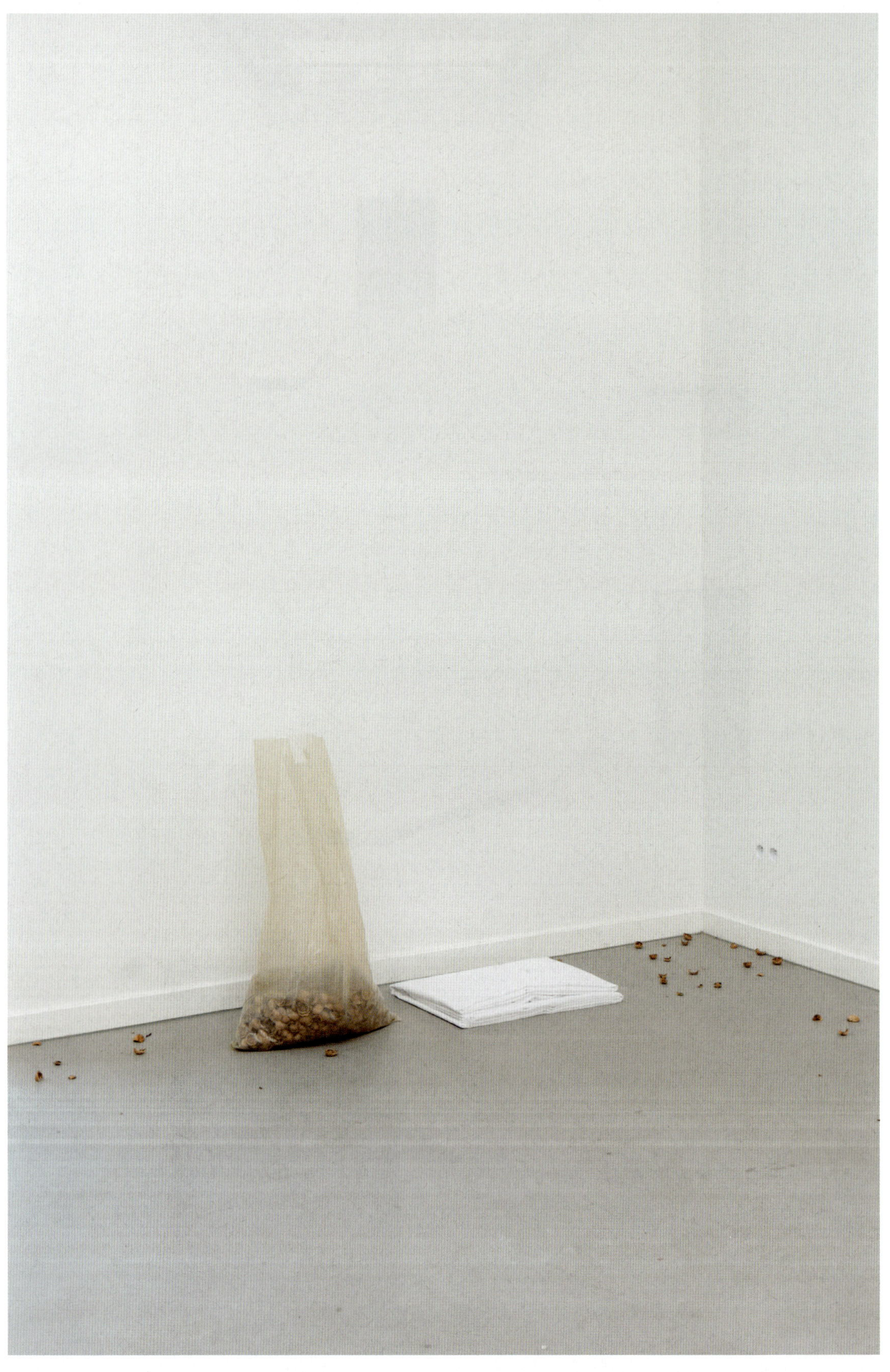

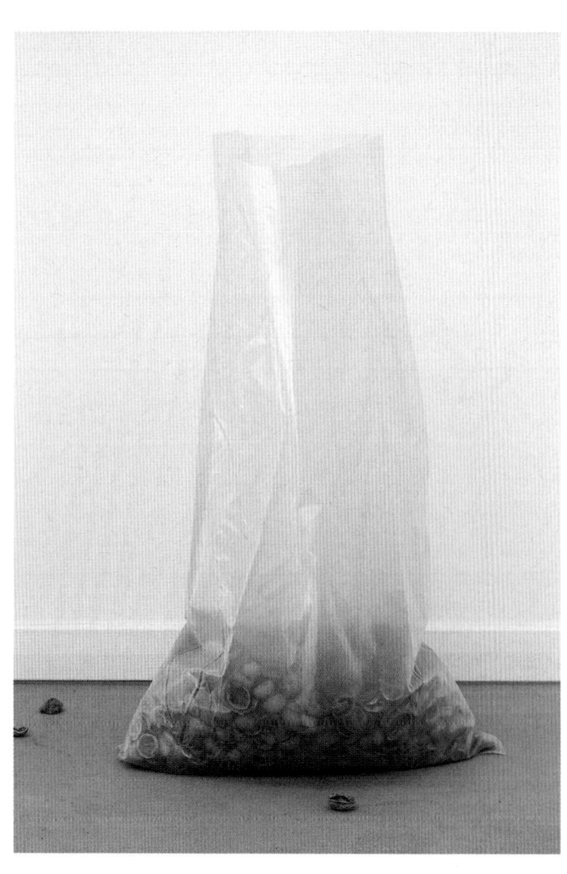

(17, 16) *Fugue*, installation view, 2025
(17) Aaron Amar Bhamra, *occasions*, 2024, walnut shells, space, various dimensions

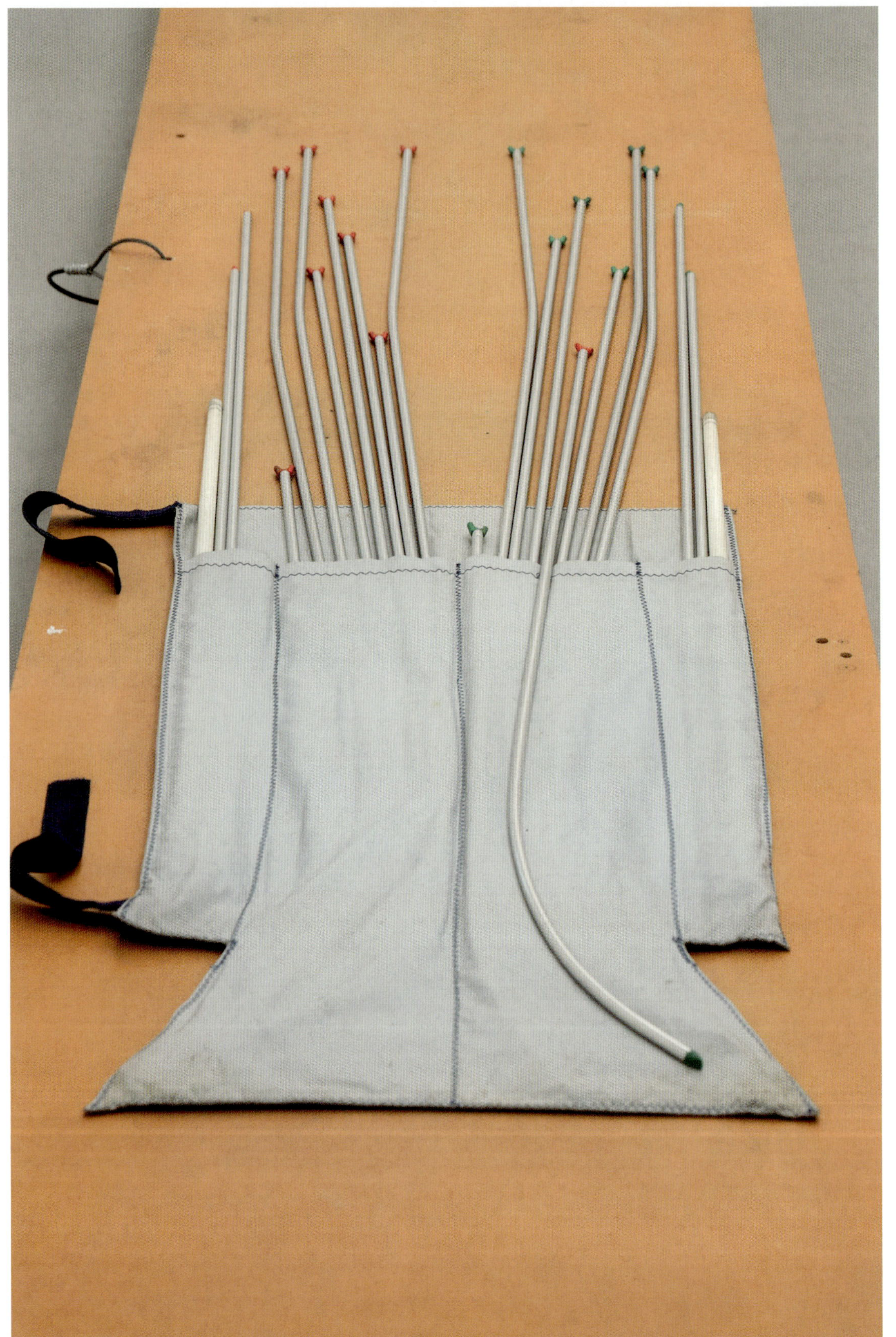

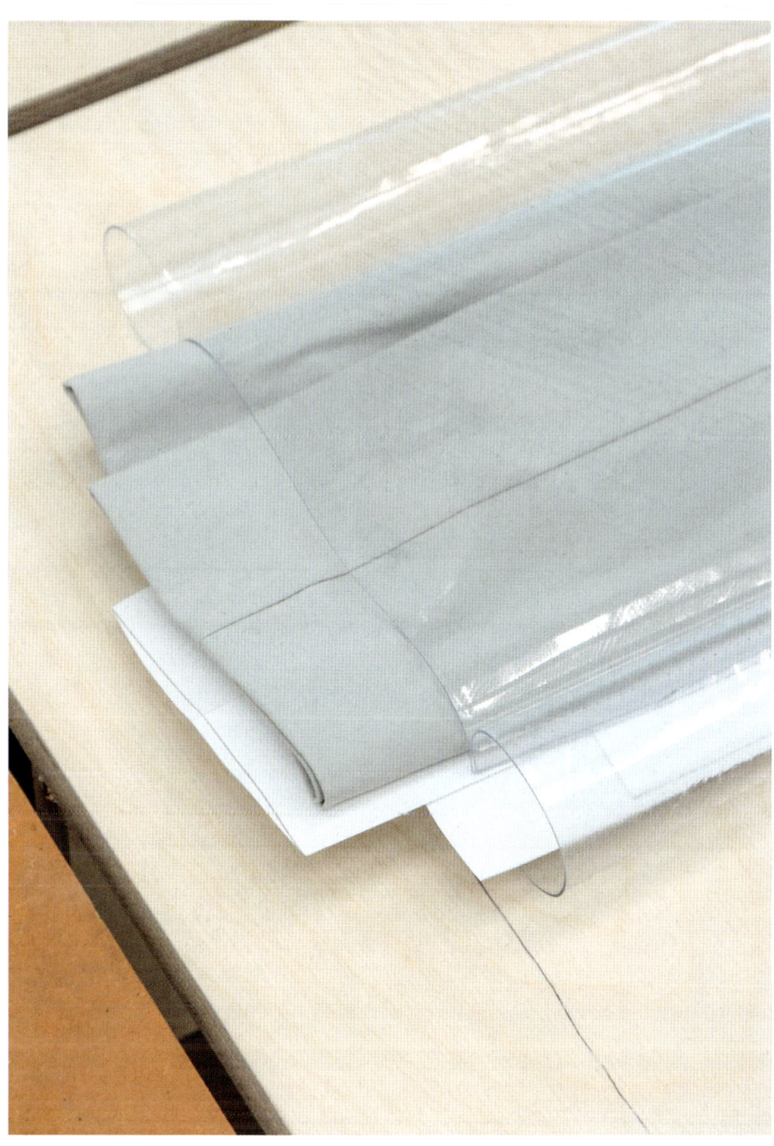

(2) Aaron Amar Bhamra, *midair*, 2025 / *Kite (sleep-like)*, 2025, various parts of an Icaro 2000 Laminar 12 (textile, threads, polyvinyl chloride; sewn by the artist's sister Naomi), pedestal formerly used in the archive as a platform for test prints at FLACC, modular display to extend the existing pedestal, 500 × 40 × 21 cm / 200 × 51 × 1,5 cm / various dimensions (details)

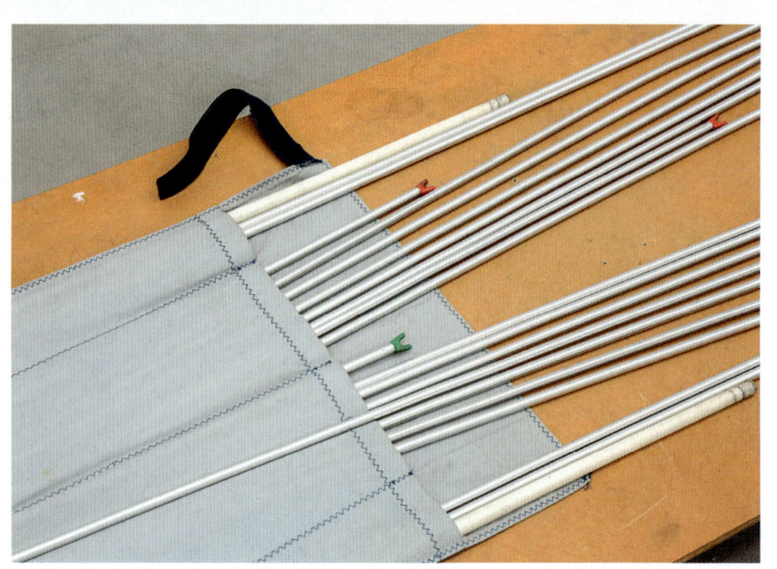

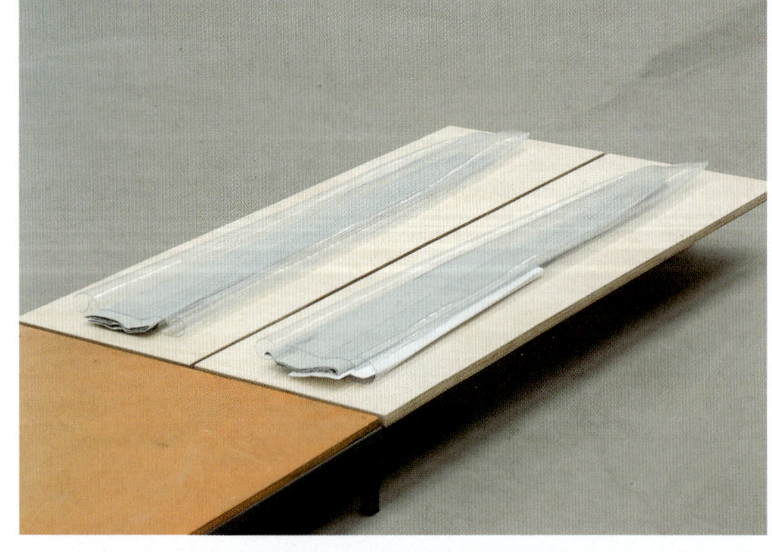

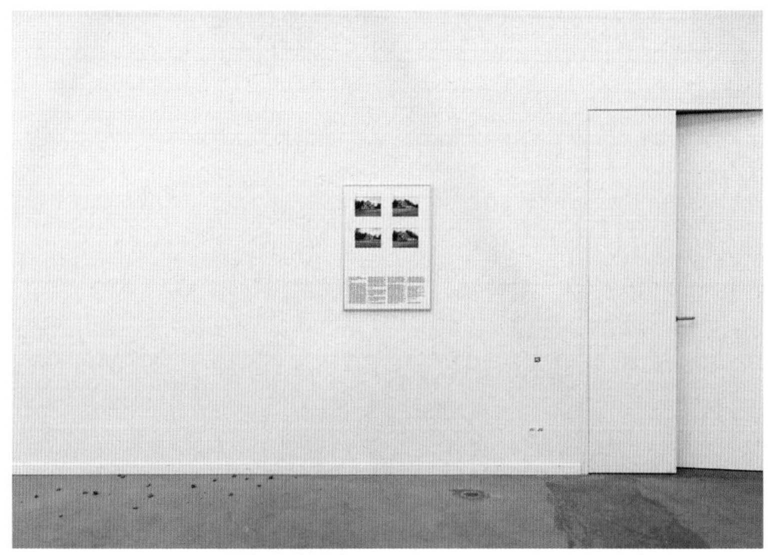

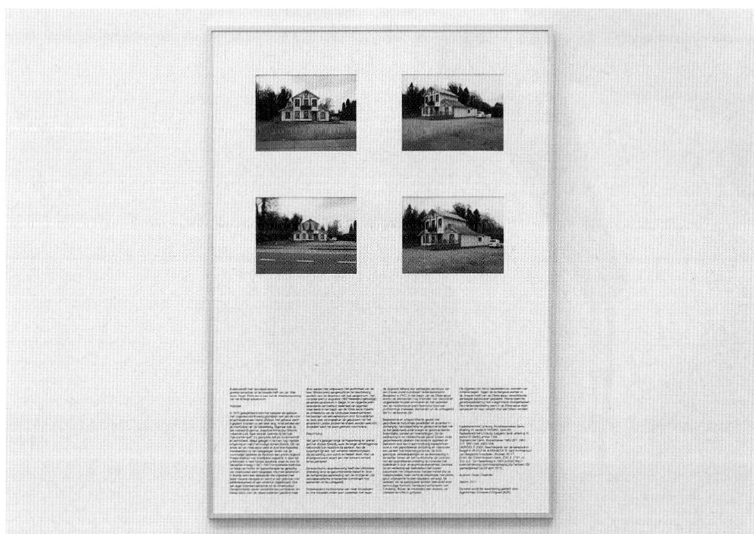

(2) Aaron Amar Bhamra, *miduir*, 2025 / *Kite (sleep-like)*, 2025 (details)
(13) Céline Mathieu, *Kneipp*, 2025, architectural heritage inventory text and images by Charlotte Foxer of the Kneipp sanatorium director's mansion used for its evocative qualities, graphic design by my friend Matt Hinkley, aluminum frame with UV-glass by Stef Renard

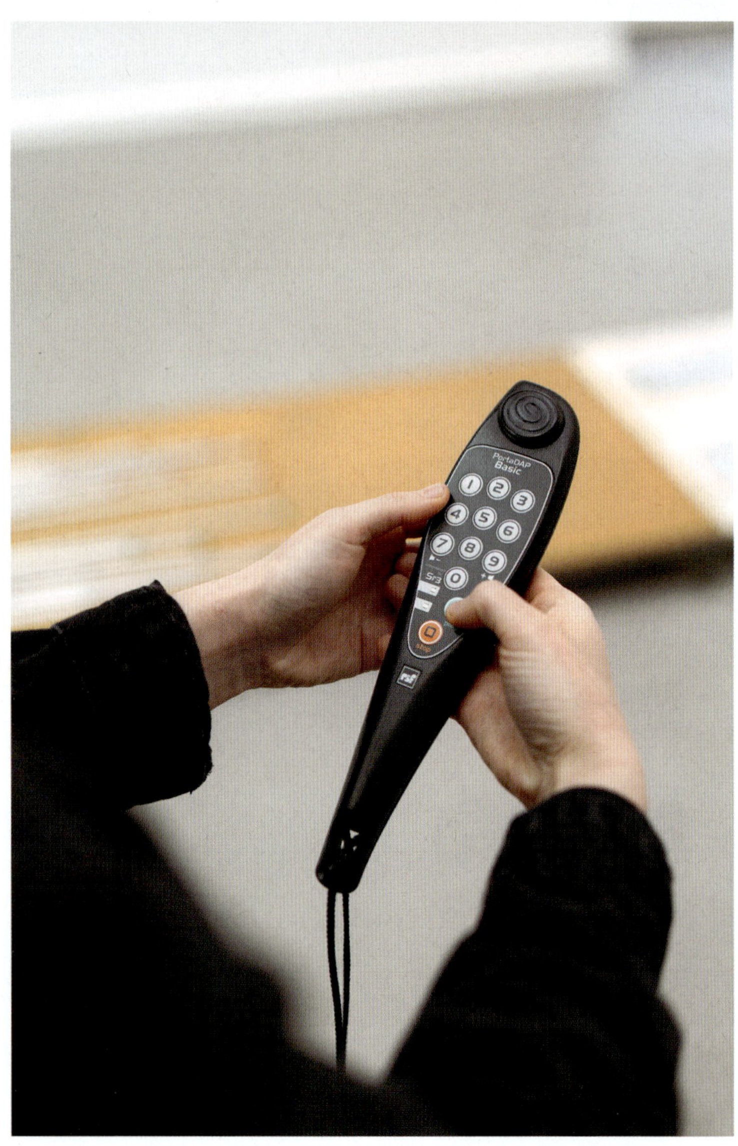

Audio guide, voice and text by Céline Mathieu, 2025
(2, 8, 20, 13, 16, 17) *Fugue*, installation views, 2025

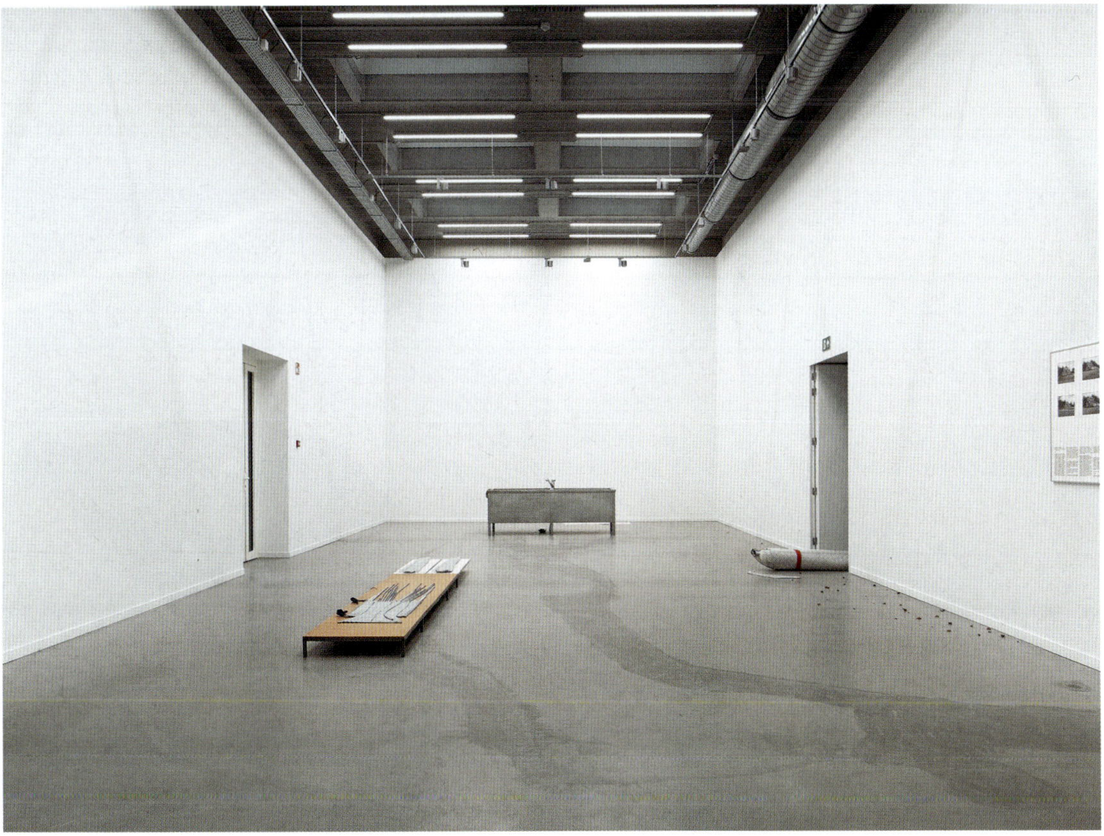

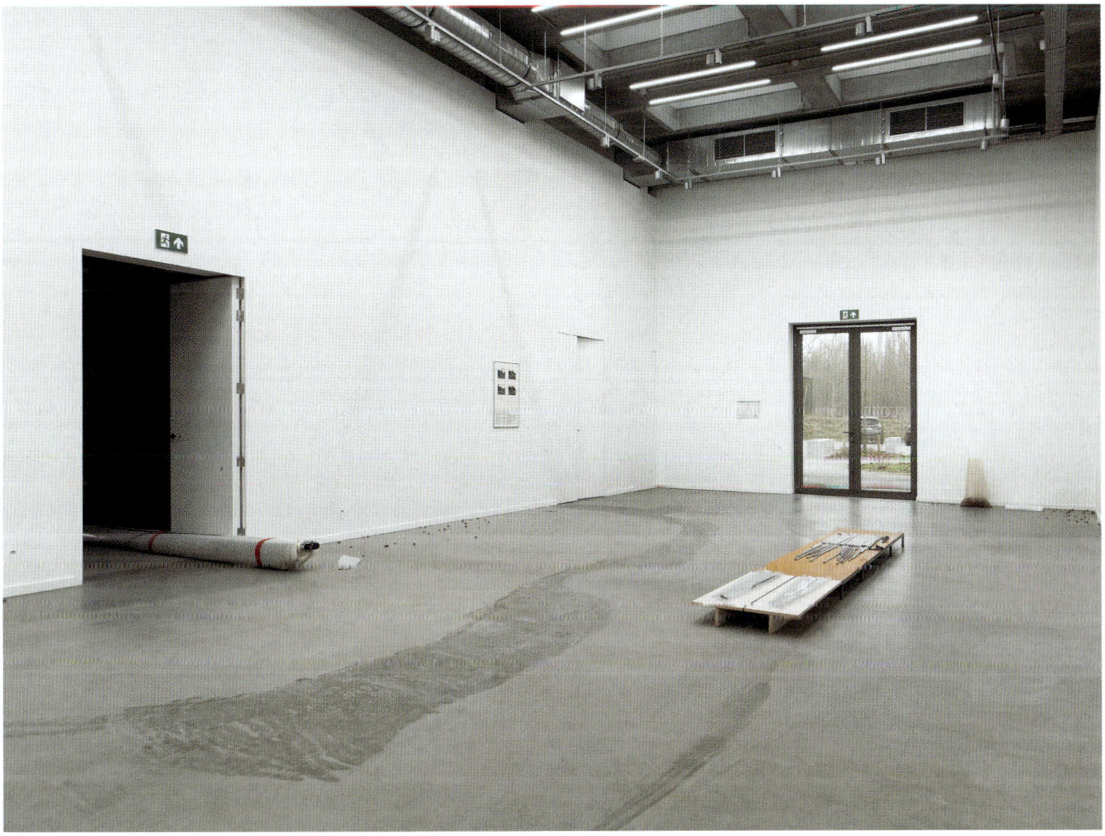

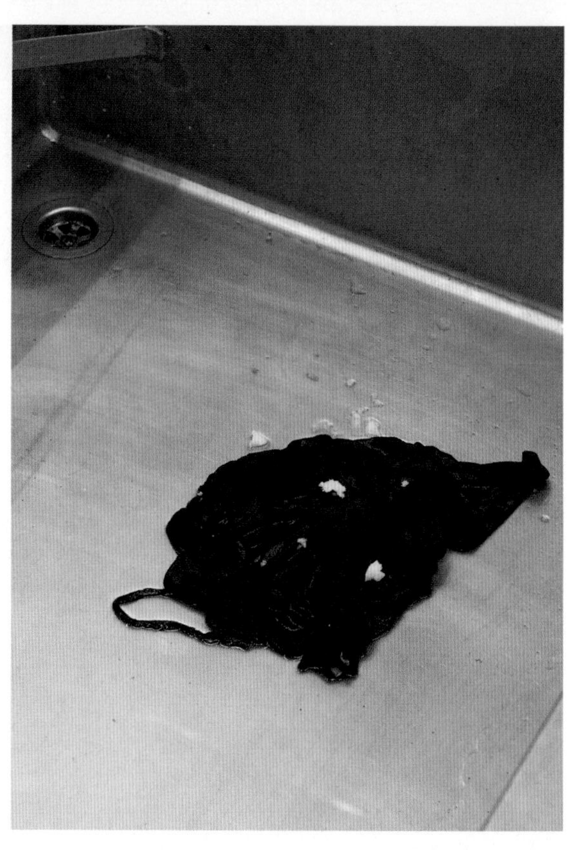

(8) Céline Mathieu, *Bekken*, 2025, dysfunctional sink, friend Joëlle's silk shirt, her mention of it sounding like a piece of mine, coconut oil feeding the silk

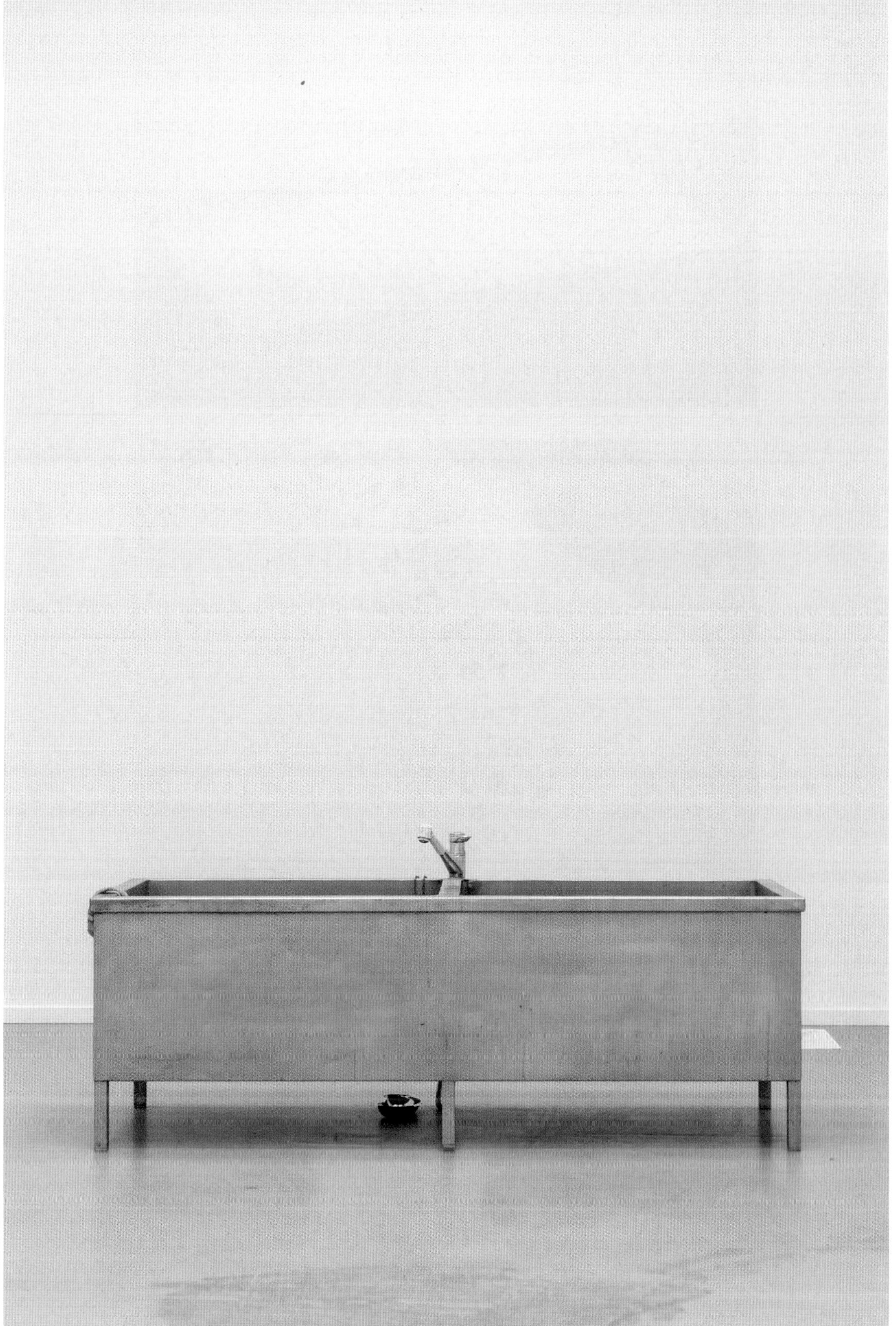

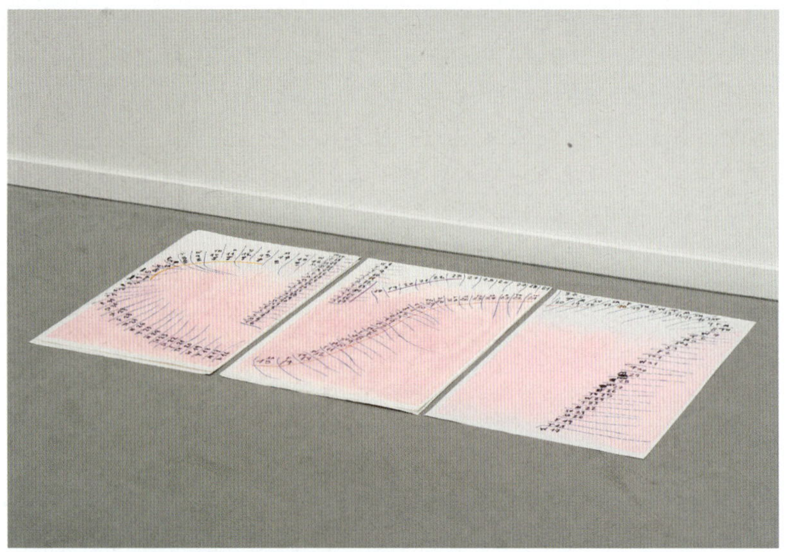

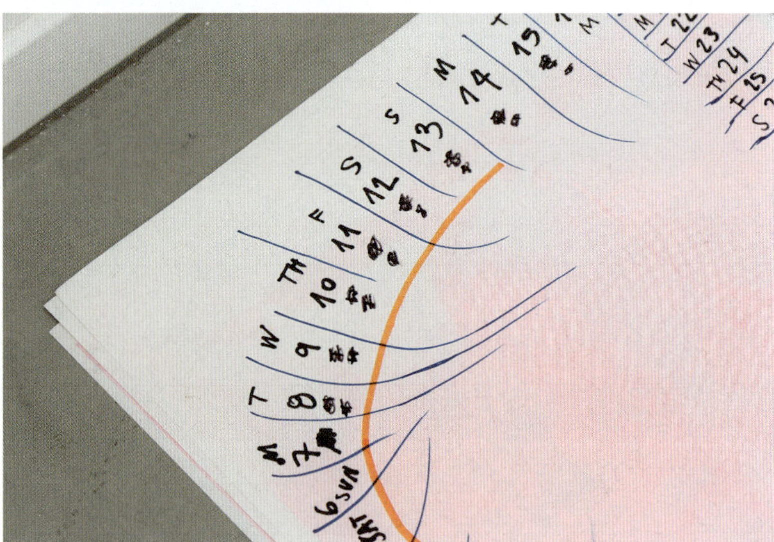

(20) Céline Mathieu, '', 2025, calendar for daily use drawn by my friend Andrea Zavala Folache visualising what time looks like in her head–valued and presented as an artwork
(2) Aaron Amar Bhamra, *midair*, 2025 / *Kite (sleep-like)*, 2025 (detail)
(7, 21, 2) *Fugue*, installation views, 2025

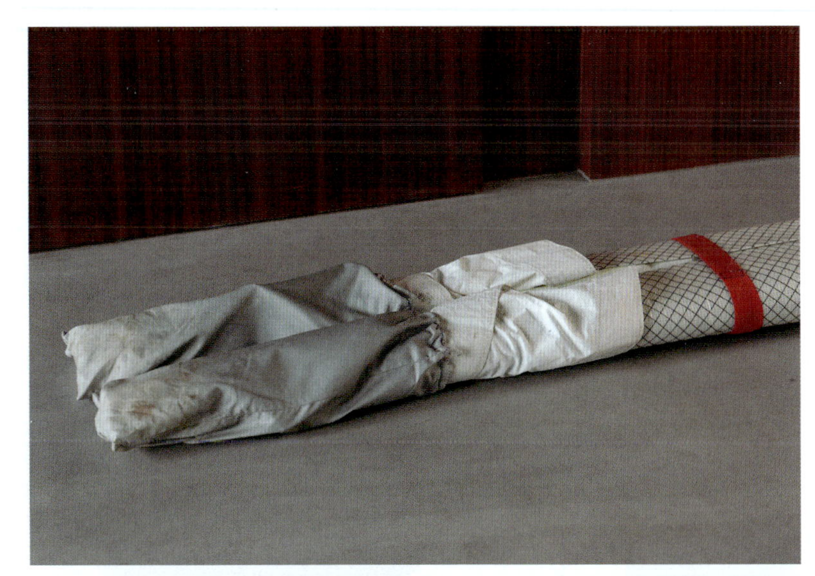

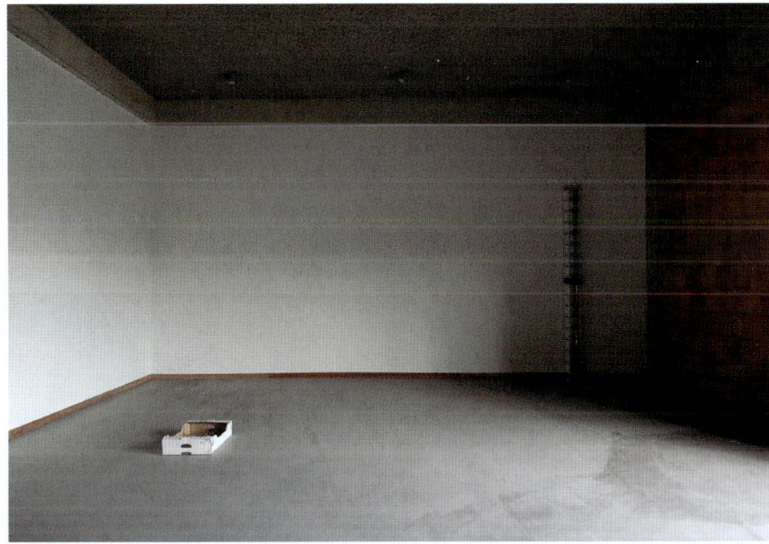

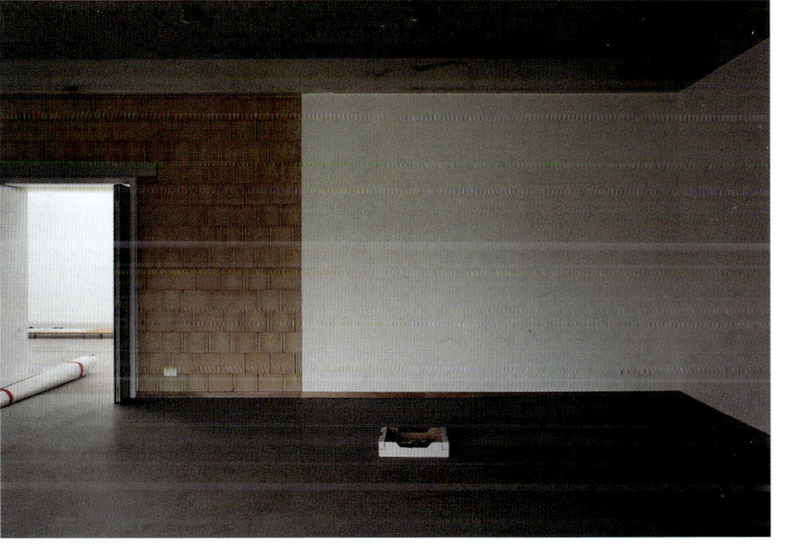

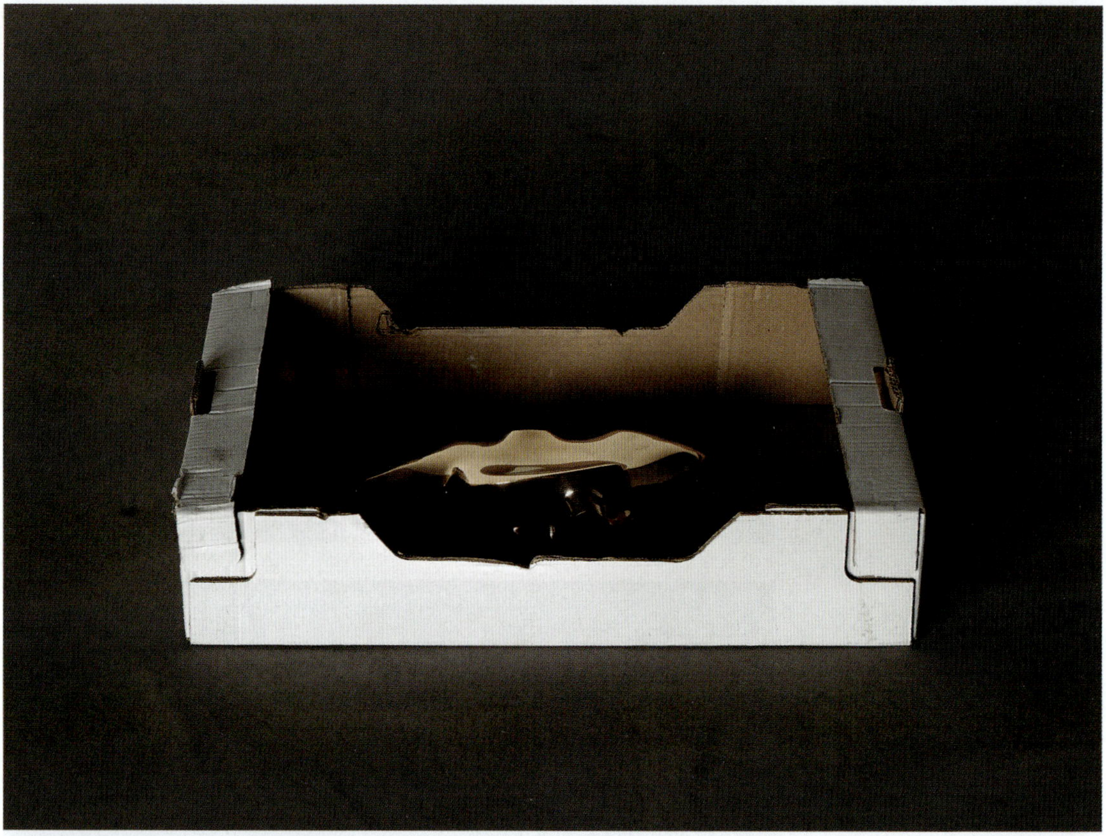

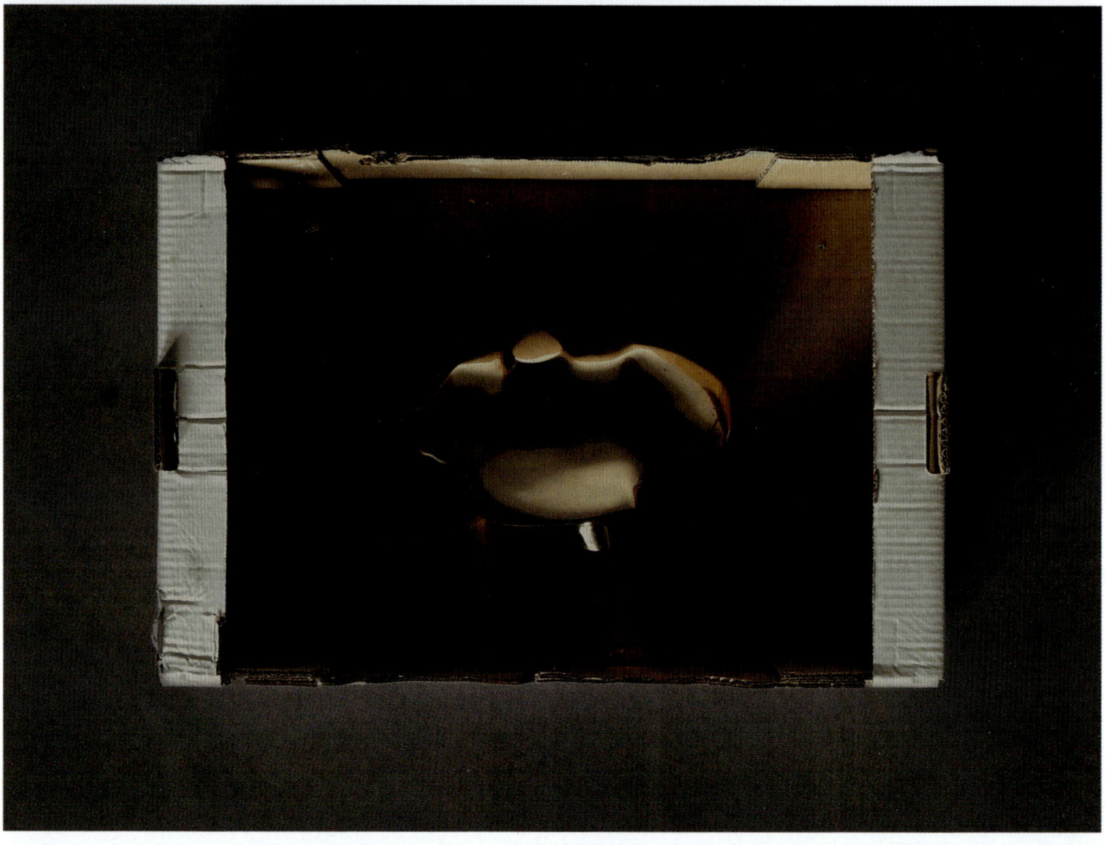

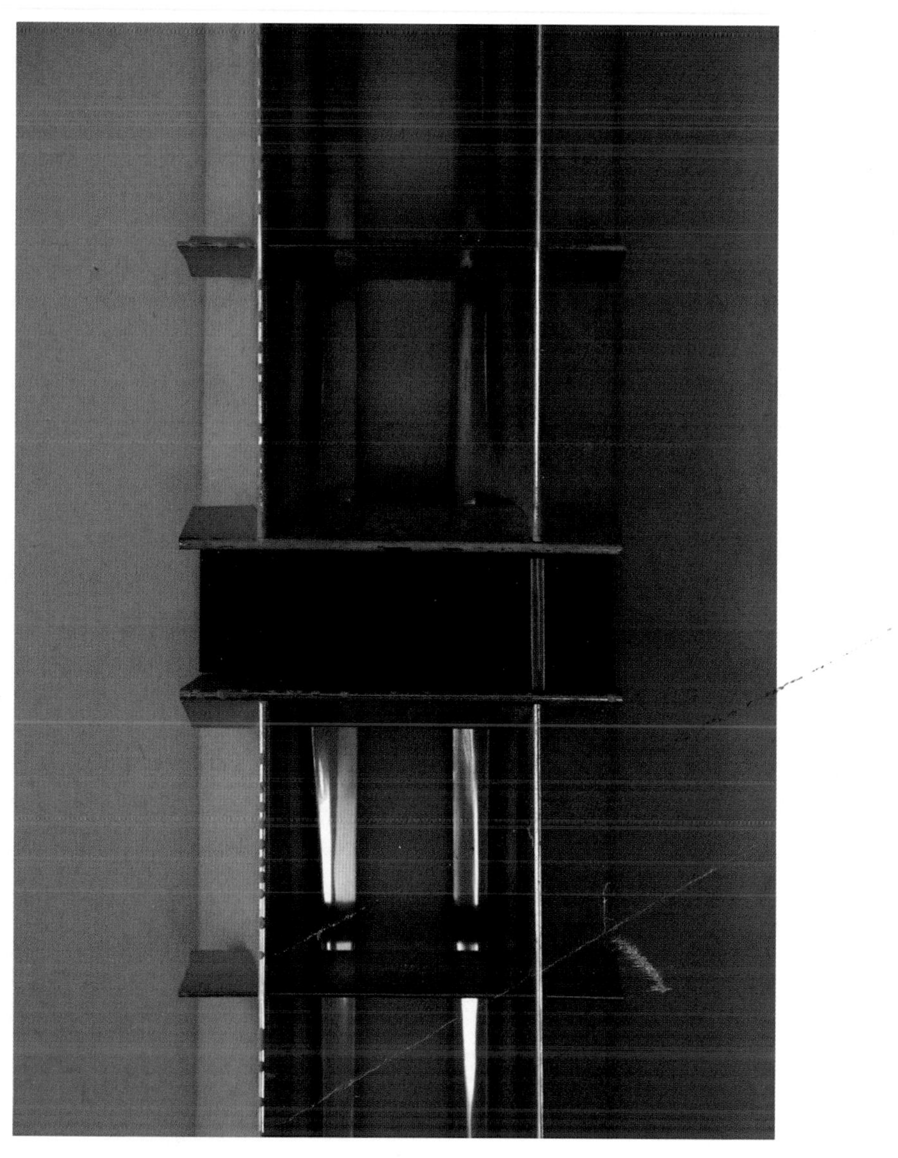

(7) Aaron Amar Bhamra, *form*, 2013–2014/2025, polished bronze, 32 × 18 × 9 cm
(21) Aaron Amar Bhamra, *lamp covers (2/2)*, 2020–2021/2025, aluminum, steel, acrylic paint, wood, glue, staple, (former: *untitled*, 2022, two ceiling lights from another space, 248 × 18 × 6 cm) 257 × 23,5 × 14 cm (detail)

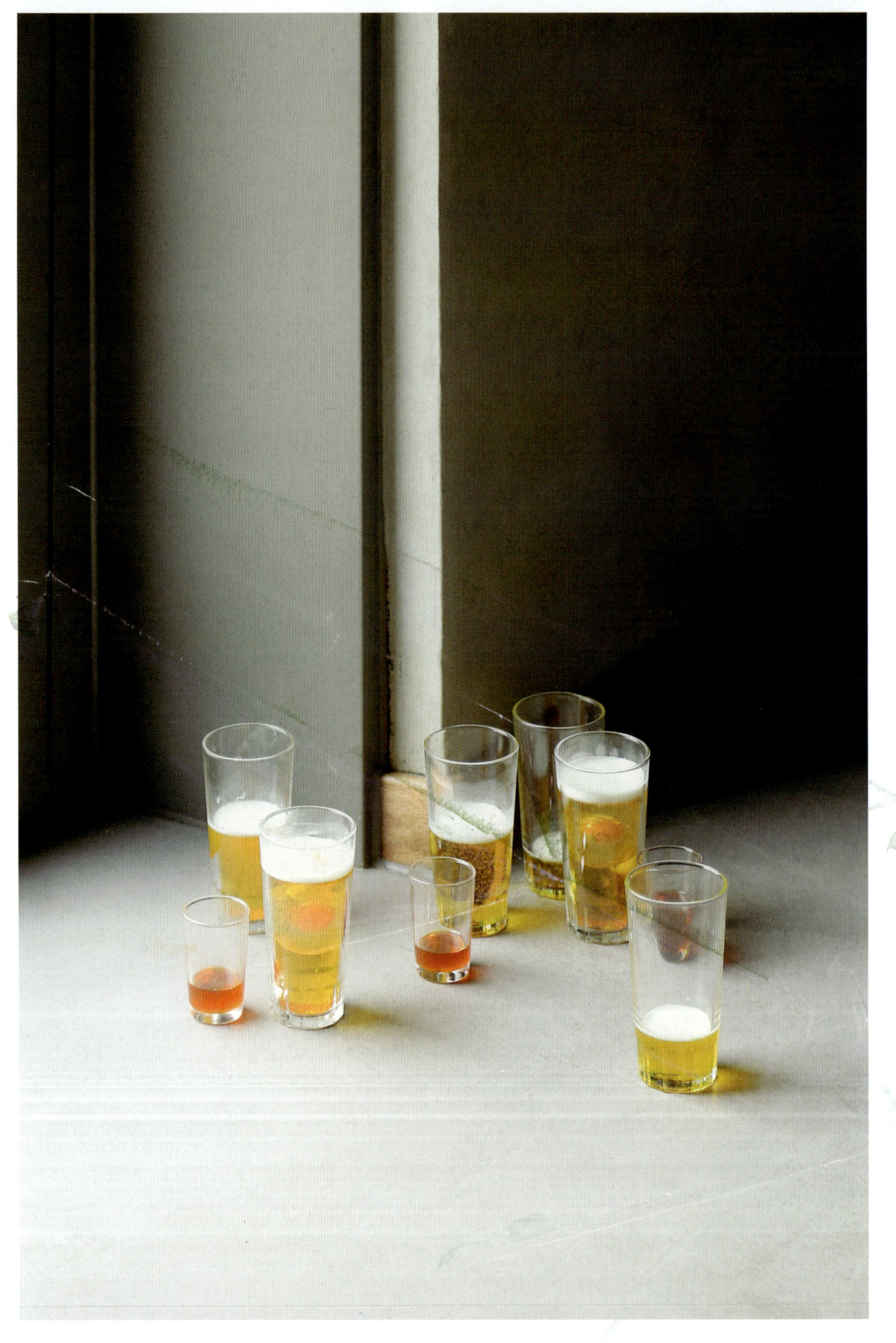

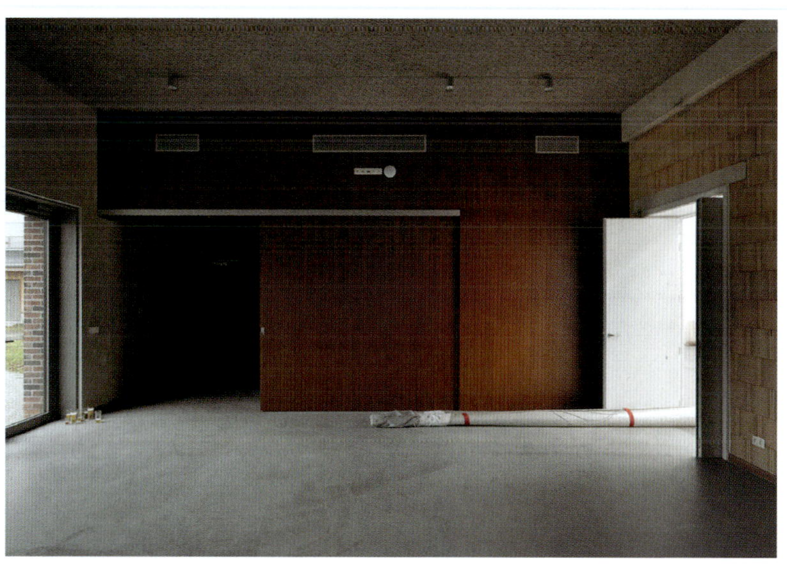

(5) Céline Mathieu, *Miners' Breakfast*, 2024, 3D-printed UV-cured eggs, two-component epoxy resin beer and whiskey imitations, technical skills of sculptors Kasper De Vos and Mathias MU exchanged for writing application texts, courtesy of the collection of Luc Haenen
(5, 2) *Fugue*, installation view, 2025

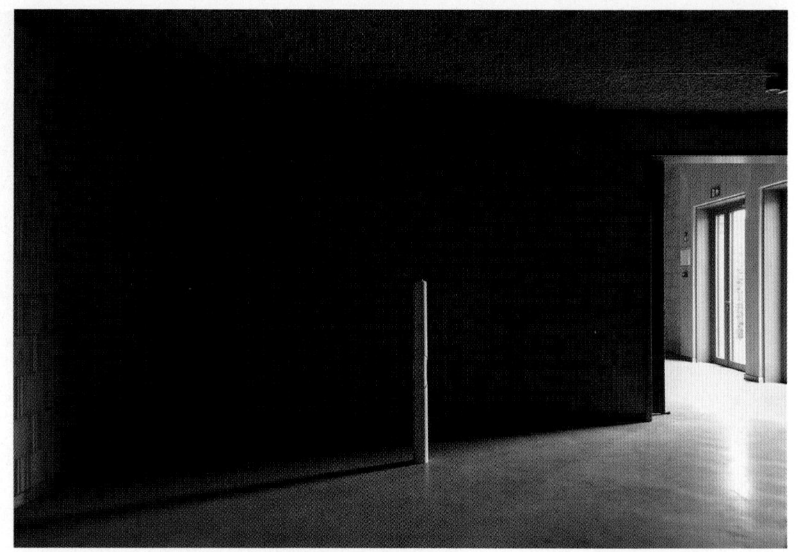
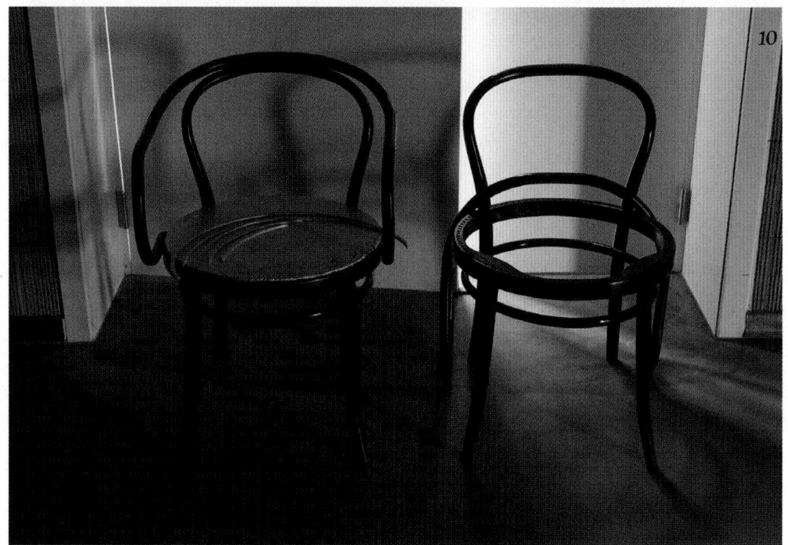

(14) Aaron Amar Bhamra, *Lime-white ceiling*, 2025, paper, 136 × 16 × 16 cm
(10) Aaron Amar Bhamra, *The distance of the moon, or Don't tell me the moon is shining; show me the glint of light on broken glass*, 2025, two Thonet 209 gifted by Fridolin & Angelika, aluminum, 120 × 70 × 80 cm

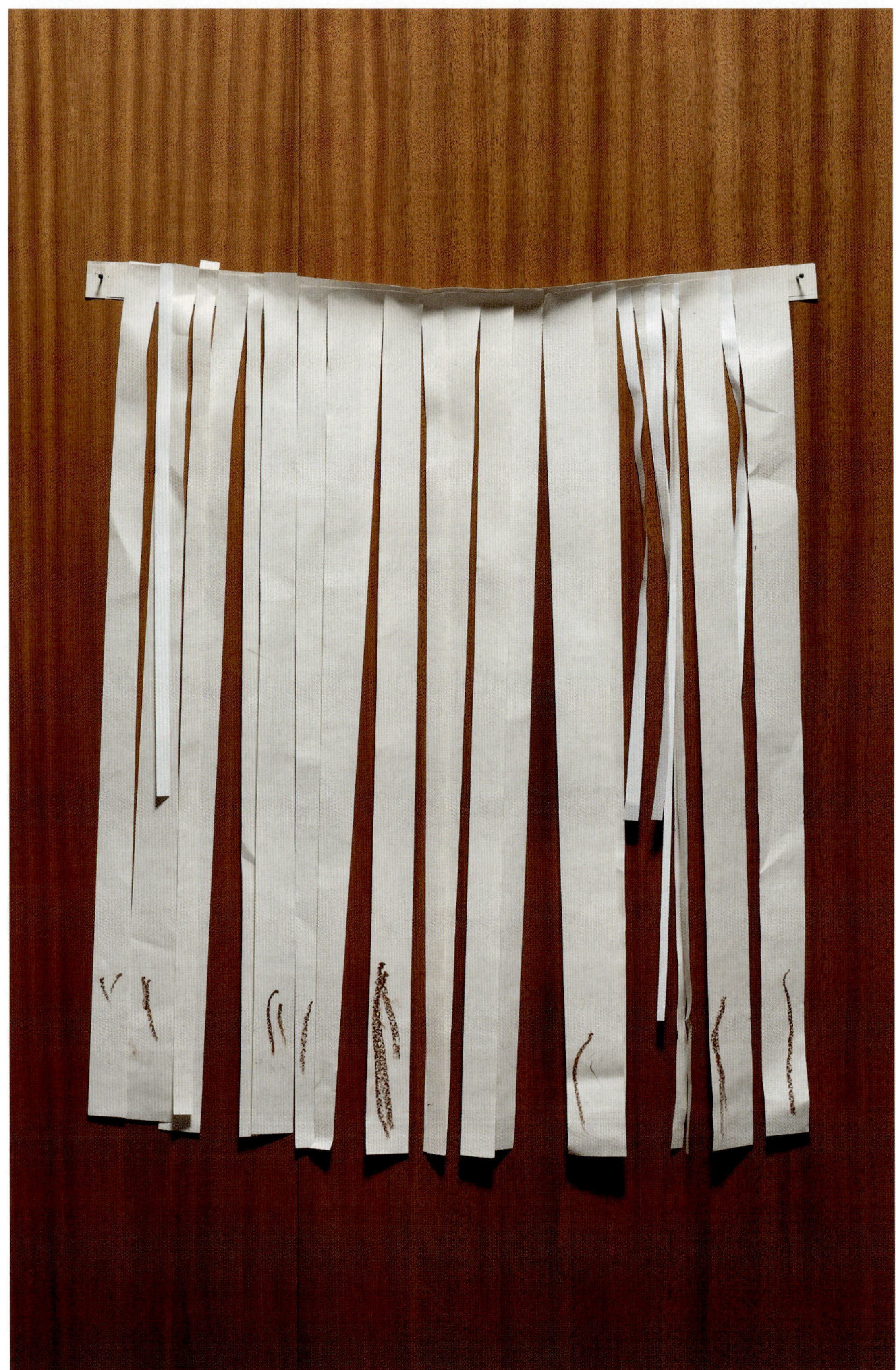

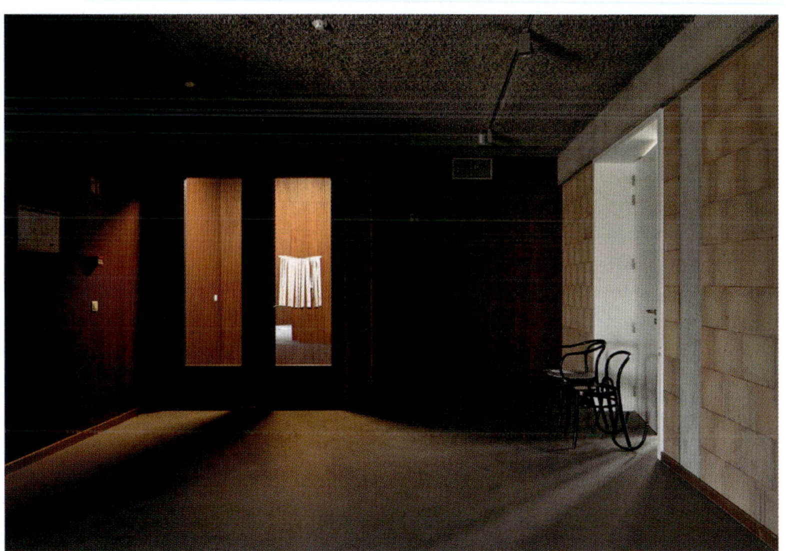

(1) Céline Mathieu, *Paper skirt scented cabin*, 2025, paper cut in strips by my friend Andrea Zavala Folache and her two-and-a-half-year-old, thoughts on how to own it without owning it, Molecule n°1 pheromone enhancing perfume on veneer (detail)
(3, 1, 10) *Fugue*, installation view, 2025
(3) Aaron Amar Bhamra, *untitled*, 2025, print on paper, (publicly accessible areas of the exhibition space of Jester, Genk) 369 m²

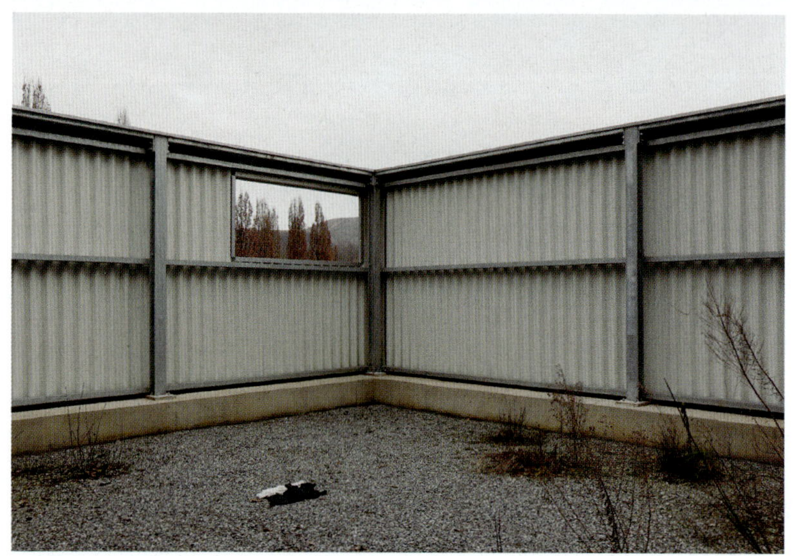

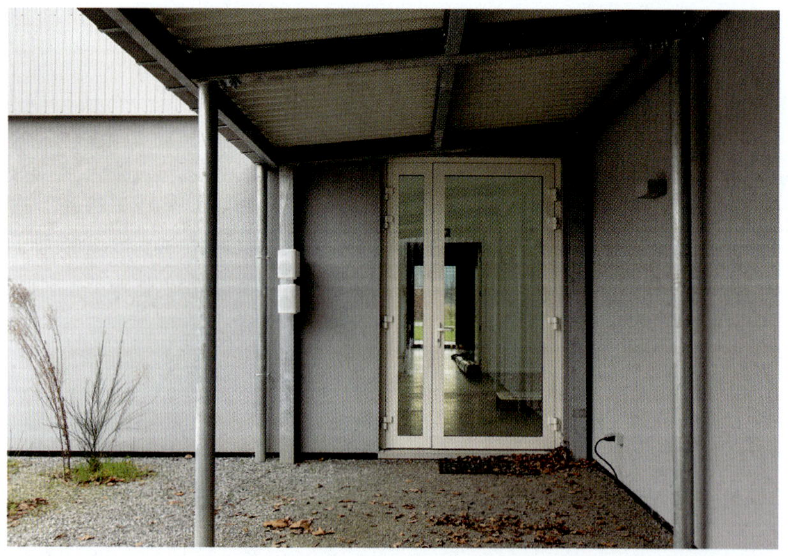

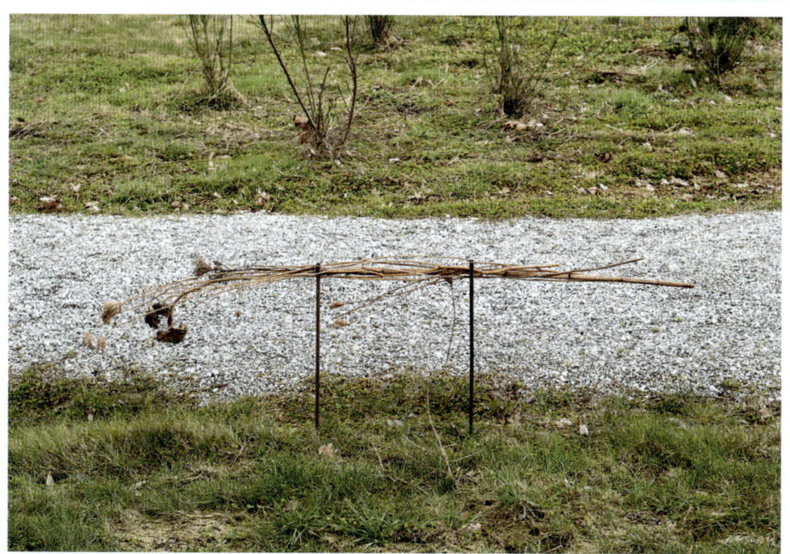

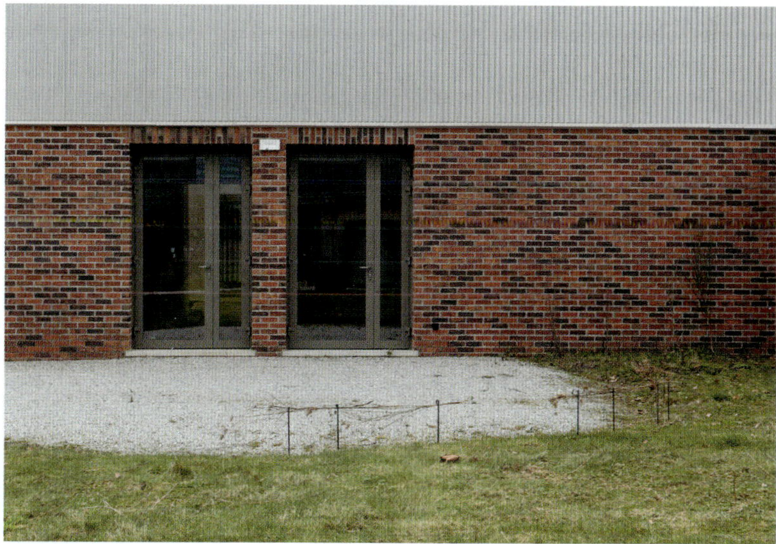

(10, 9, 12) *Fugue*, installation views, 2025
(12) Aaron Amar Bhamra, *The pressure of your palms*, 2025, steel, various dried flowers from the garden of Jester collected by Céline in autumn 2024, the sound of birds talking, various dimensions

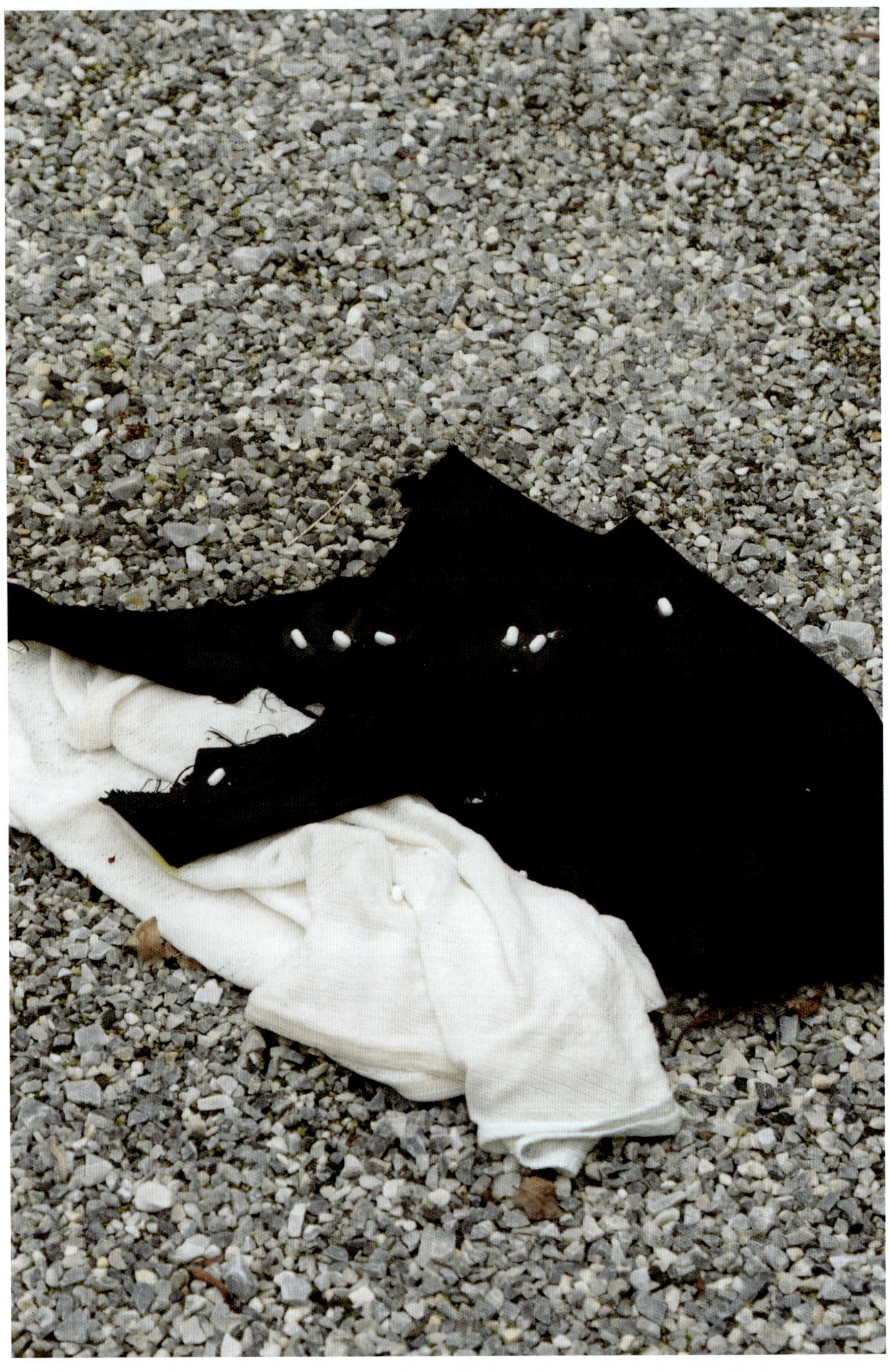

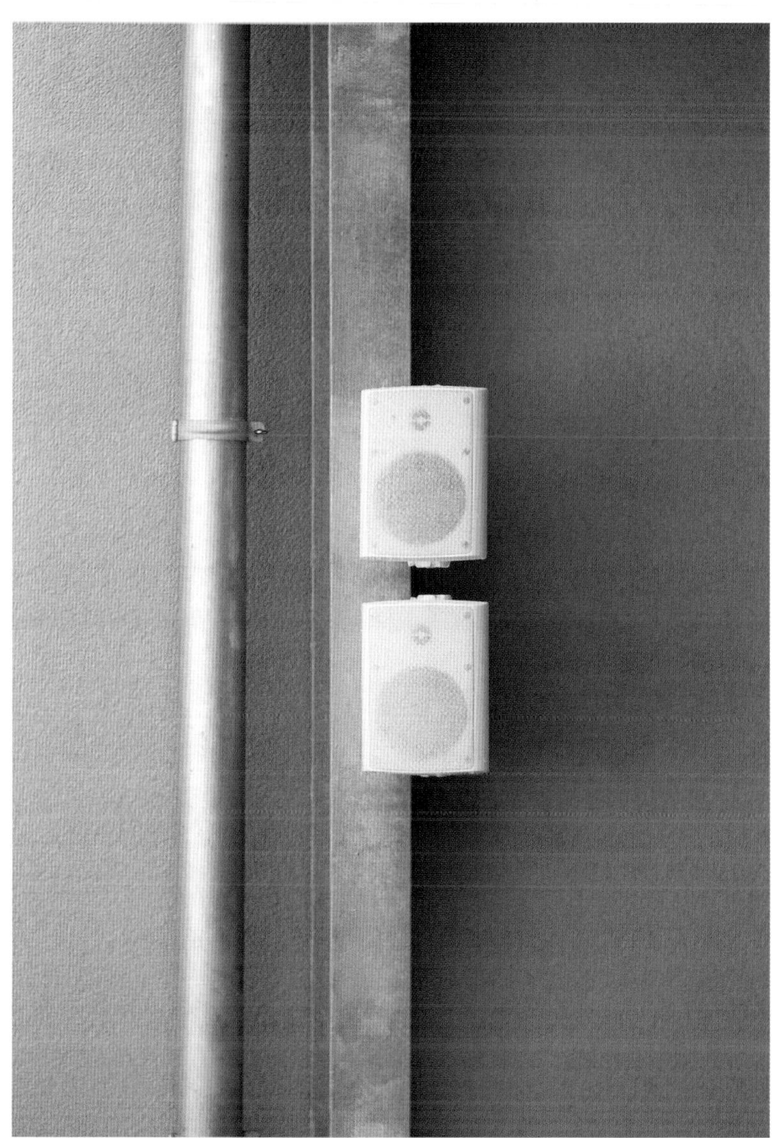

(18) Céline Mathieu, *Garments*, 2024, lower part of my cropped jacket, garment by textile chemist Rosie Broadhead (75% viscose, 20% algae, 5% elastane–viscose is derived from the cellulose of eucalyptus trees in this case, but is chemically processed to create the yarn), Tic Tac mints (detail)
(9) Céline Mathieu, *Vent / Girl harmonising with fan*, 2025, my friend Ginevra harmonising with Jester's ventilation system on my request after her referencing the YouTube video *Girl harmonising with fan*

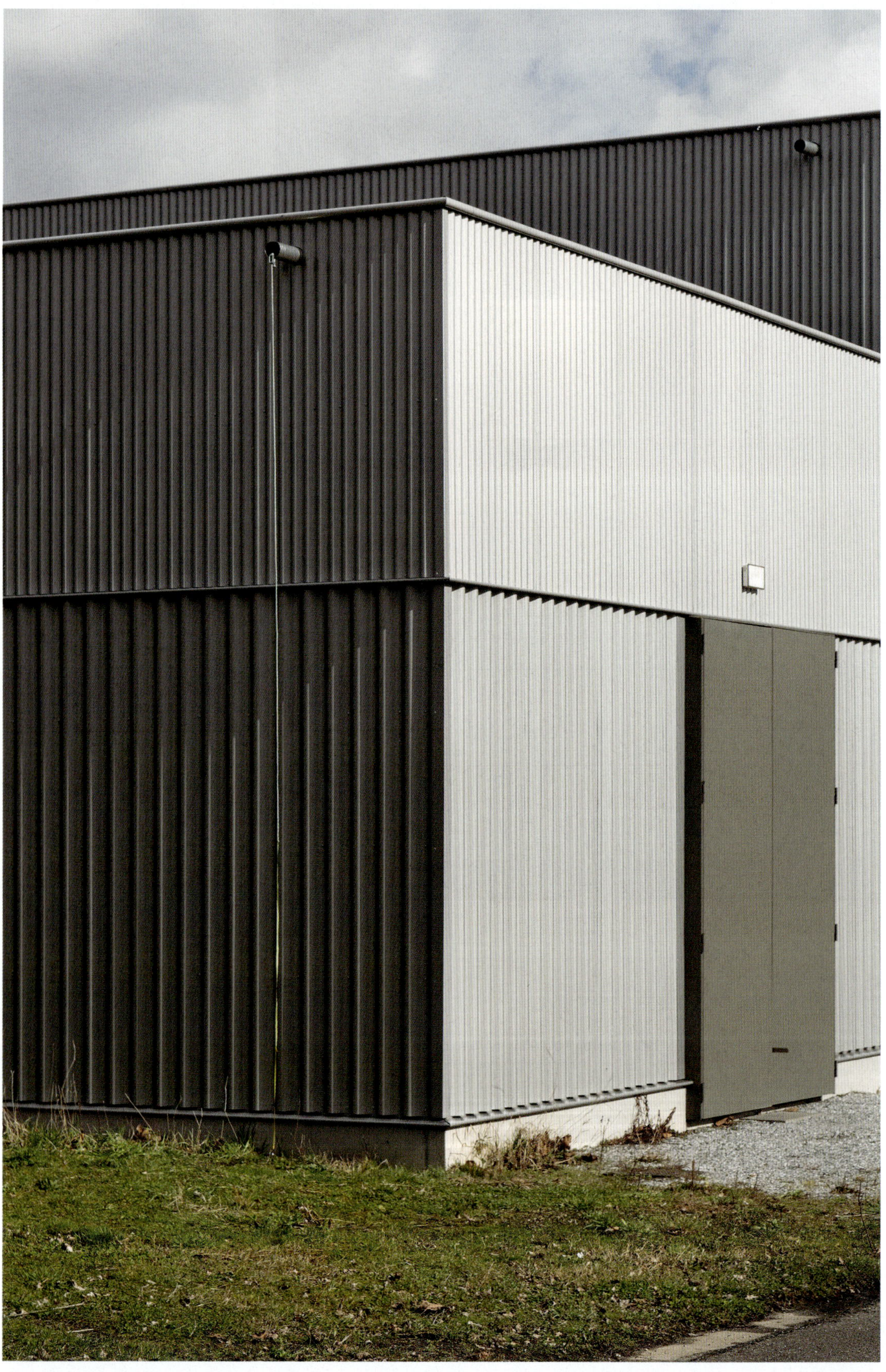

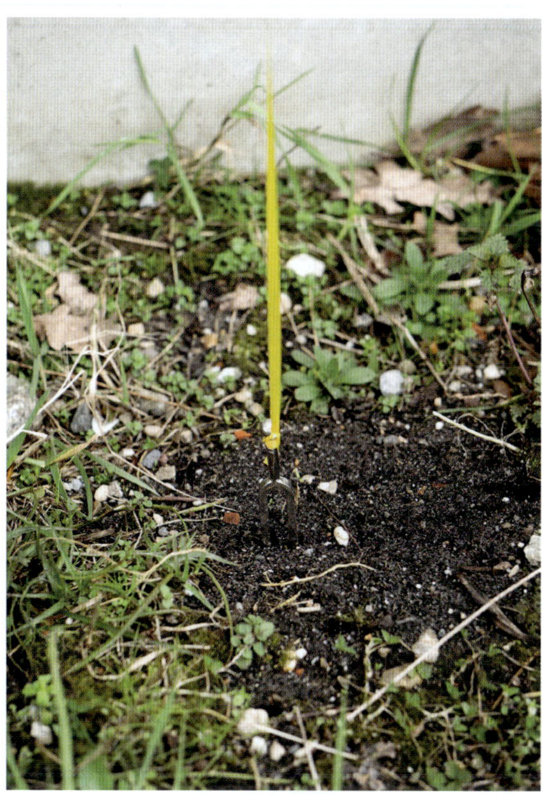

(15) Céline Mathieu, *Outdoor thread*, 2025, thread connecting the drainpipe to the floor preventing dripping sounds, inspired by a gesture of T.B.

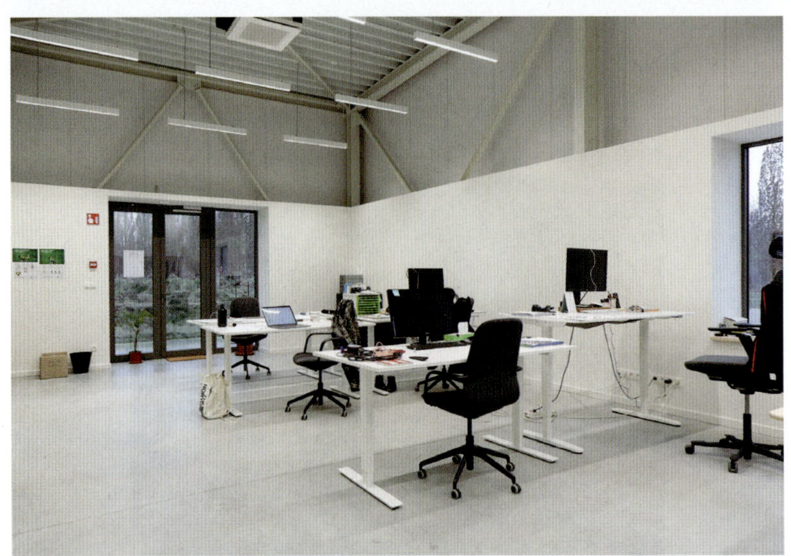

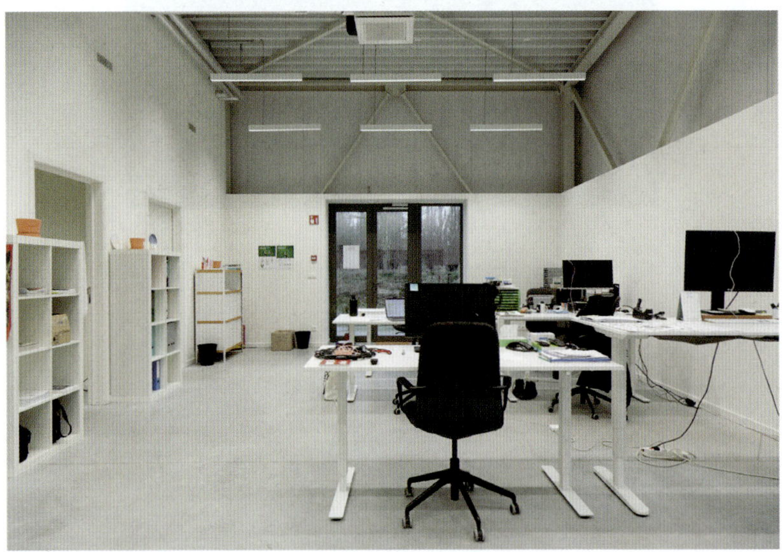

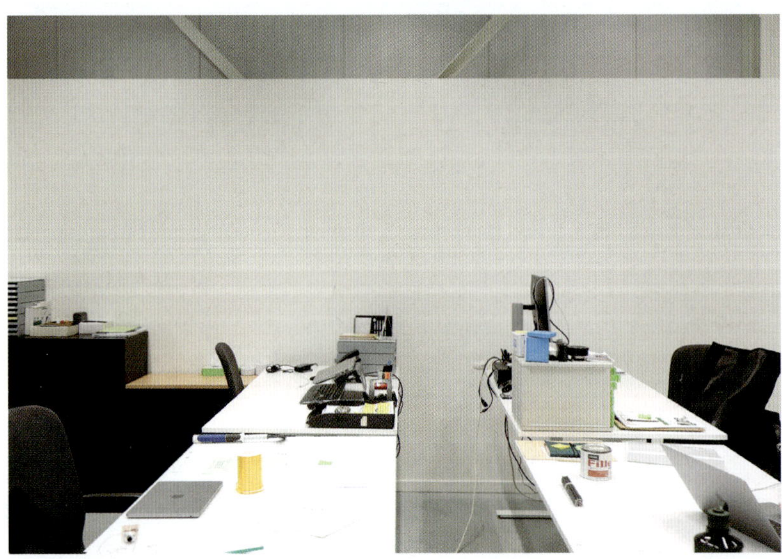

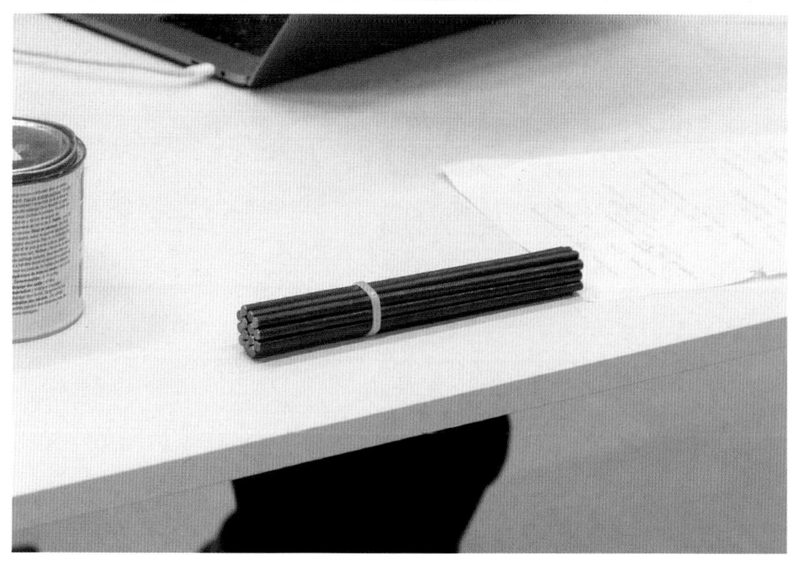

(19b, 22b) *Fugue*, installation views, 2025
(22b) Aaron Amar Bhamra, *A series of hand-sized table weights for the office building*, 2025, various materials, various dimensions

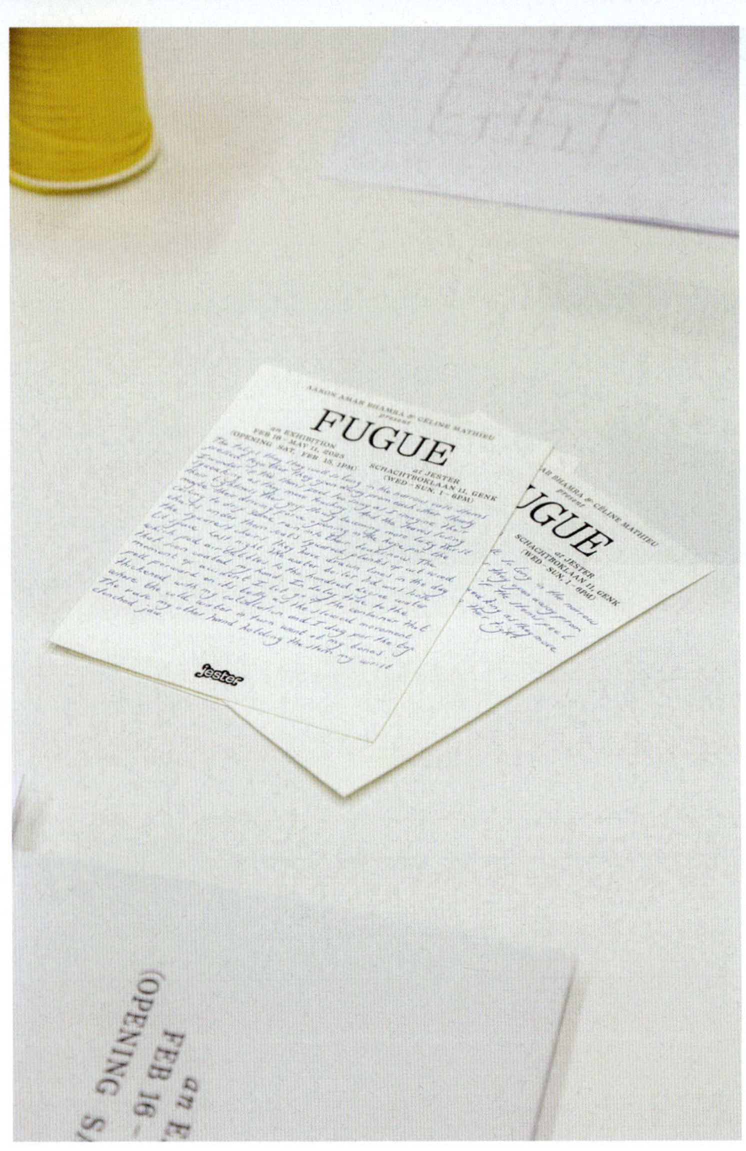

(19b) Céline Mathieu, *Tone*, 2025, a text on tulips and their thirsty beaks that I wrote last year, copied by hand by Karel and Wauthier on the white space of the *Fugue* flyer
(22b) Aaron Amar Bhamra, *A series of hand-sized table weights for the office building*, 2025

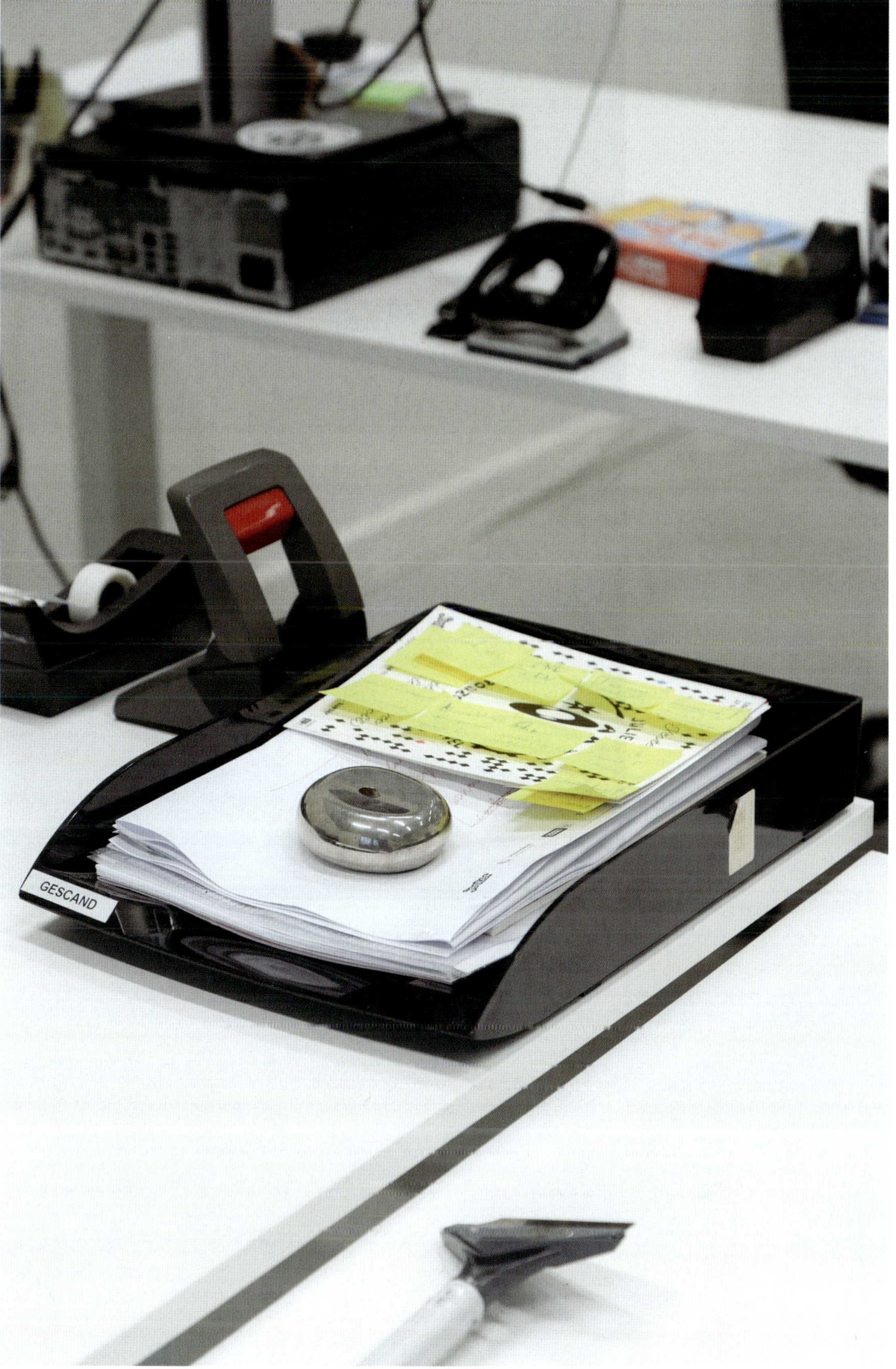
GESCAND

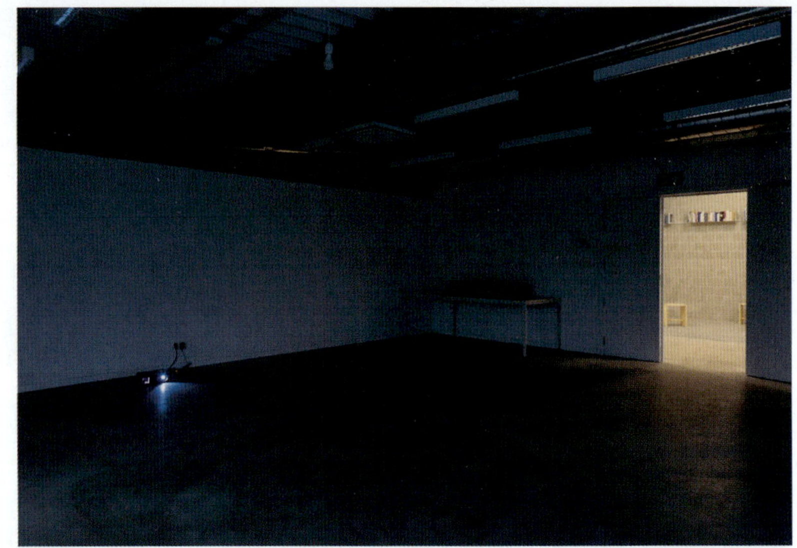

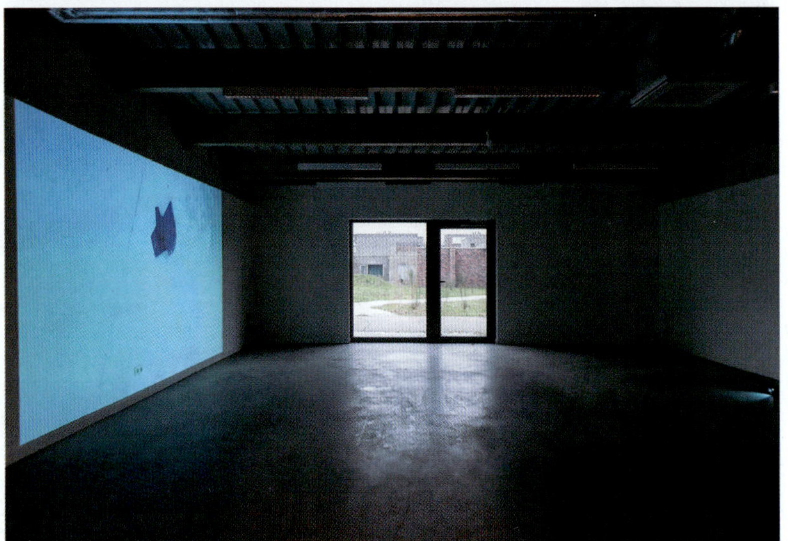

(6c) Aaron Amar Bhamra, *untitled*, 2023/2025, projection (approx. 58 seconds) on display until the arrival of the next resident, various dimensions

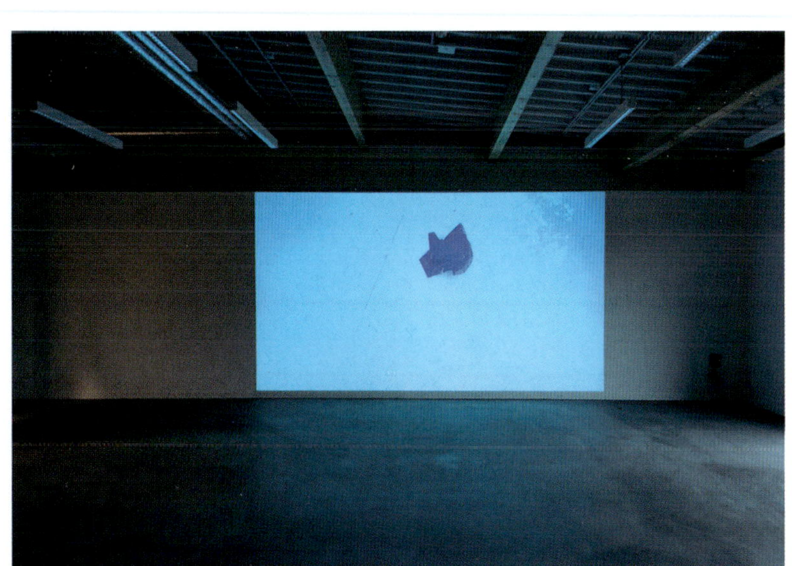

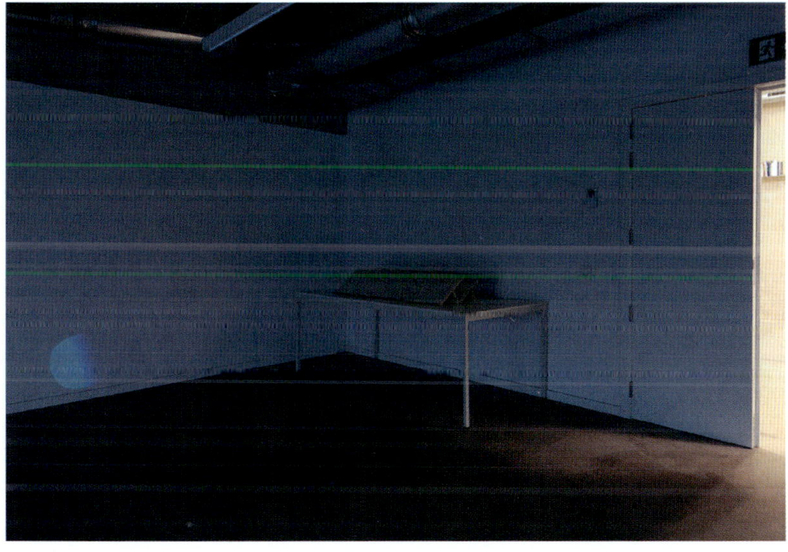

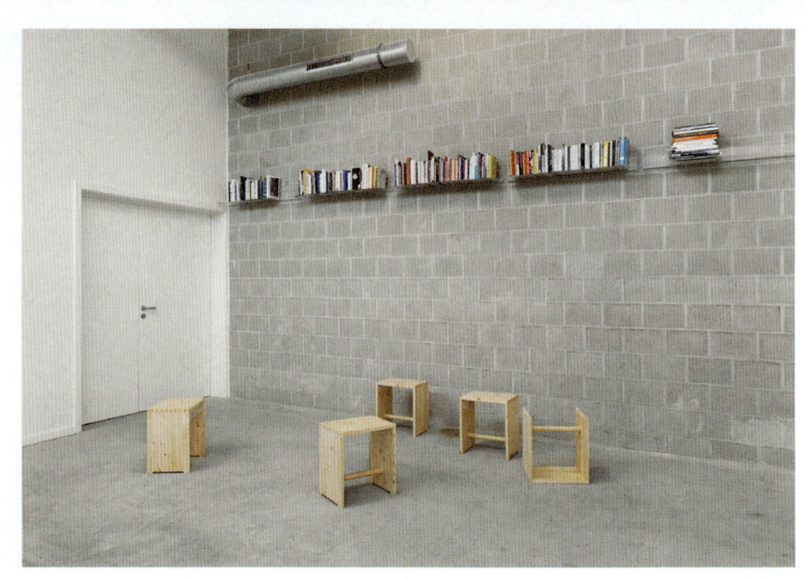

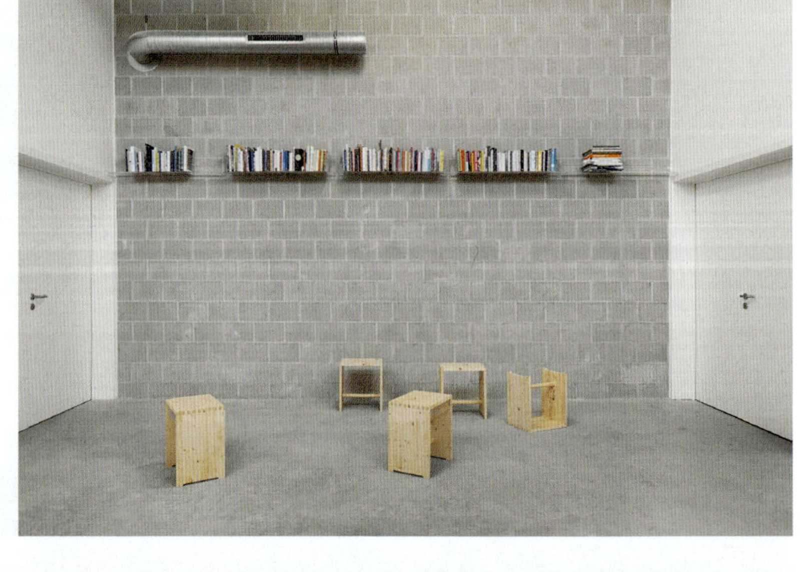

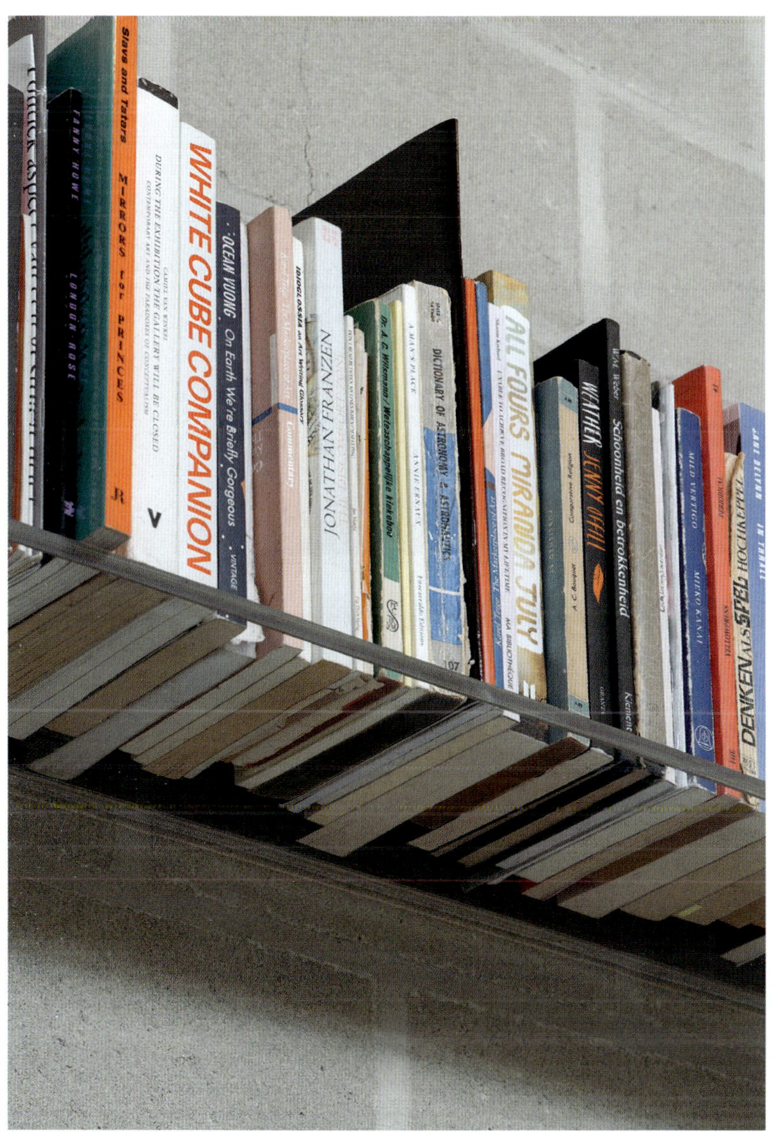

(11a) Céline Mathieu, *The Library*, 2024/2025, my personal library (exchanged for the institution's archive as a permanent work after *Fugue*), Max Bill stool adaptation (woodworkers' first exercise in Basel's carpenters education; the object being stool, seat and book carrying device), plexiglass shelves, design in collaboration with Jan Omer Fack, woodwork by craftsman Stef Renard, financed and produced by Jester, first presented at artspace celador in Brussels, circulating funds, books and services

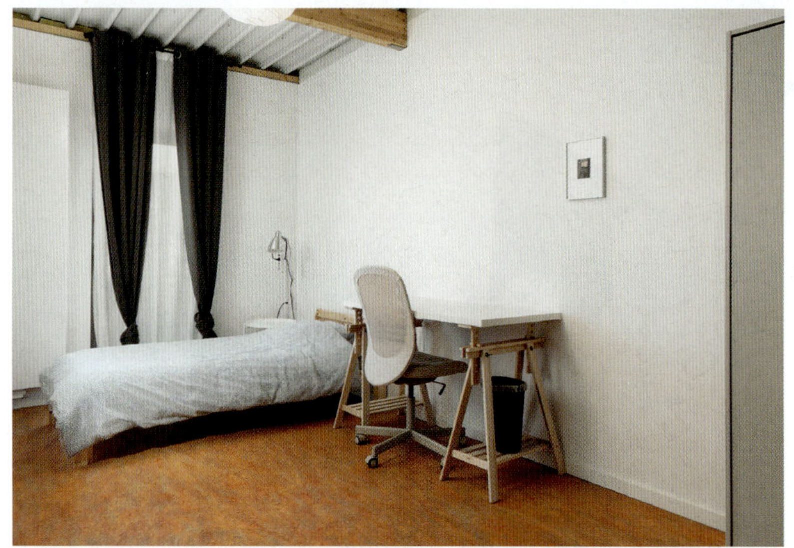

(4c) Aaron Amar Bhamra, *imagine birds talking (1-4)*, 2025, print on paper, aluminum frame, 21 × 29,7 cm
NEXT SPREAD: (23) Aaron Amar Bhamra, *anti-collision oiseaux*, 2025, bird silhouettes on the cars of Koi Persyn & Karel Op 't Eynde, various dimensions

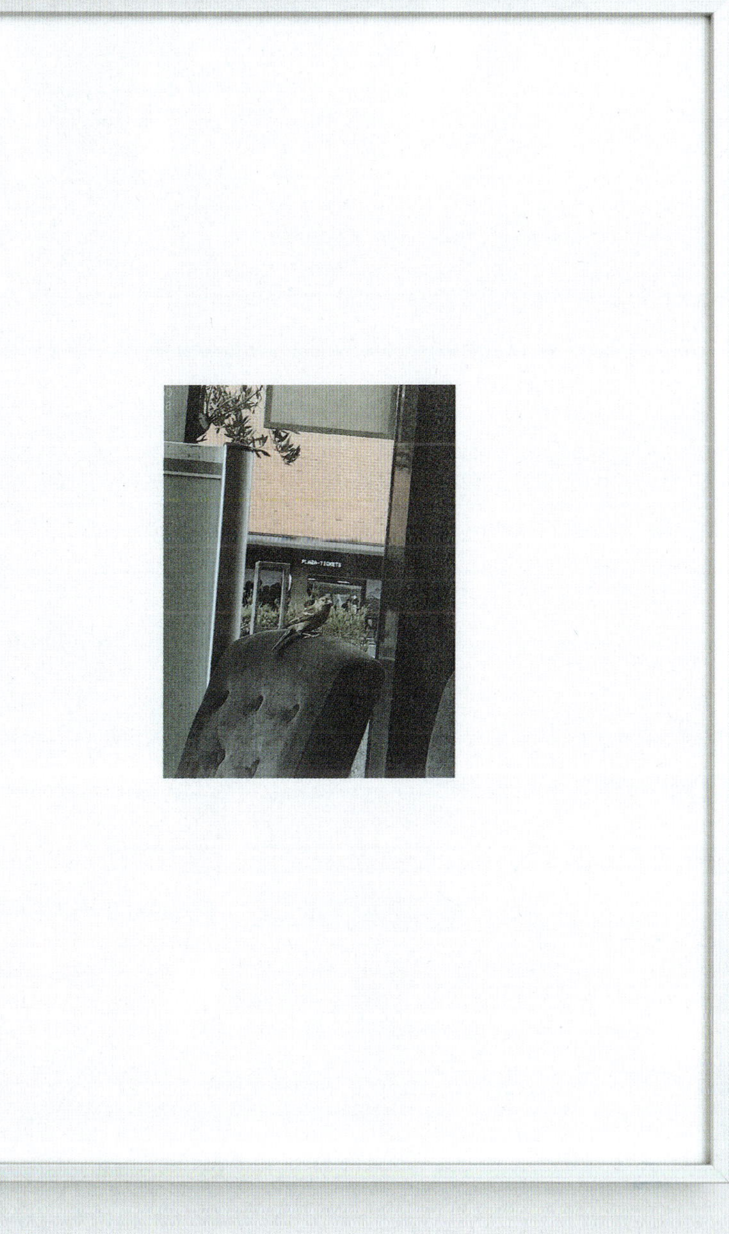

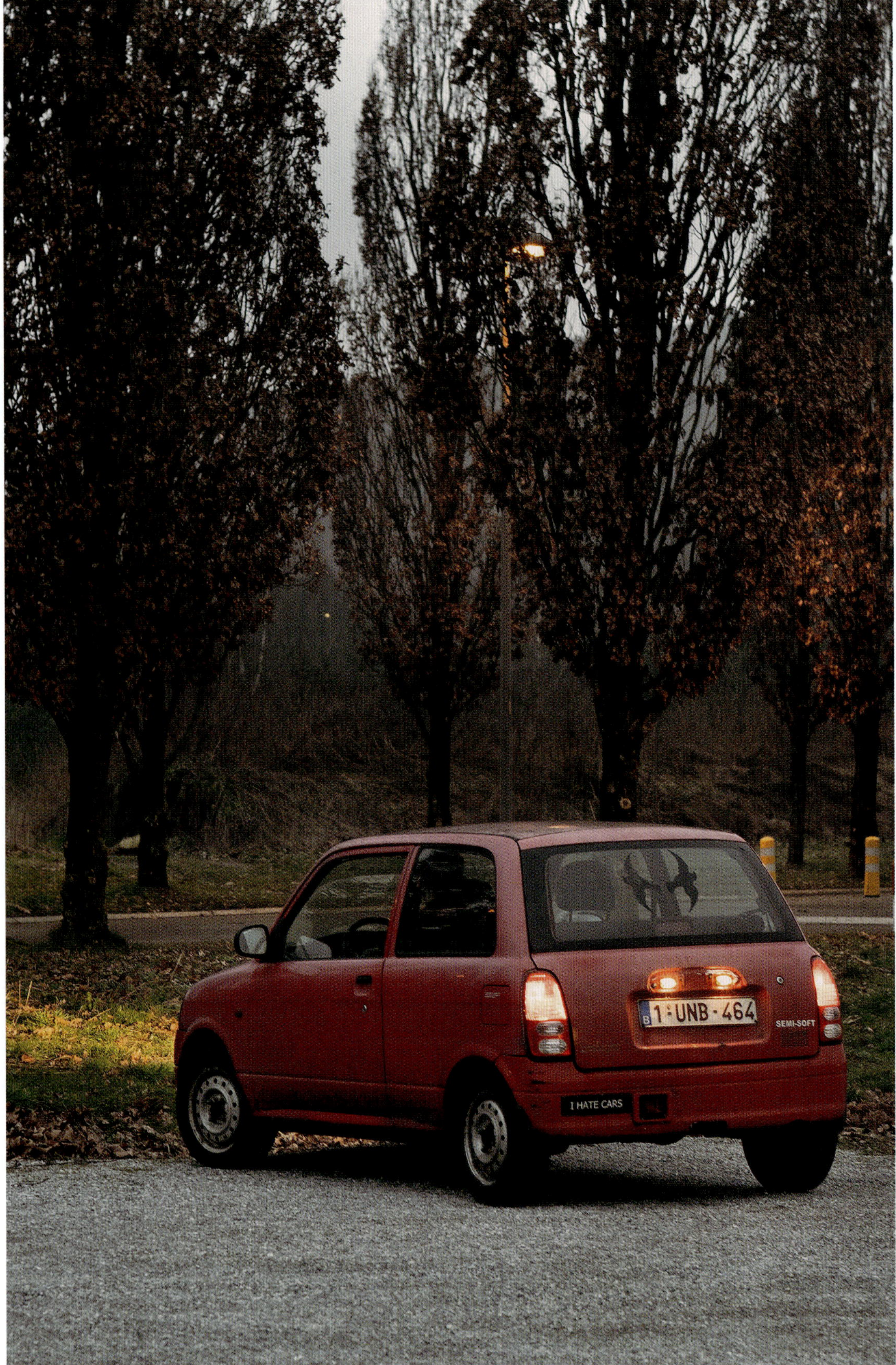

1 · UNB · 464
B
SEMI-SOFT
I HATE CARS

Aaron Amar Bhamra & Céline Mathieu     FUGUE

11a
Céline Mathieu, *The Library*, 2024/2025,
my personal library (exchanged for the institution's archive as a permanent work after
Fugue), Max Bill stool adaptation (woodworkers' first exercise in Basel's carpenters education;
the object being stool, seat and book carrying
device), plexiglass shelves, design in collaboration with Jan Omer Fack, woodwork by craftsman
Stef Renard, financed and produced by Jester,
first presented at artspace celador in Brussels,
circulating funds, books and services

6c
Aaron Amar Bhamra, *untitled*, 2023/2025,
projection (approx. 58 seconds) on display until
the arrival of the next resident, various dimensions
    23a
Aaron Amar Bhamra, *anti-collision oiseaux*,
2025, bird silhouettes on the cars of Koi Persyn
& Karel Op 't Eynde, various dimensions

a. Works on view on Wednesdays and Thursdays
b. Works on view for the employees of Jester
c. Works on view for the residents of Jester

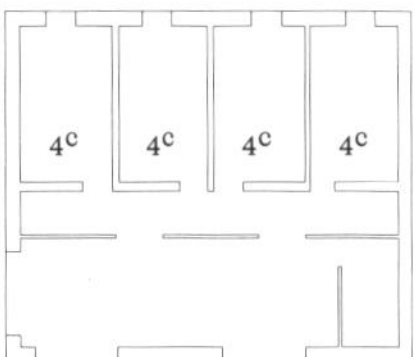


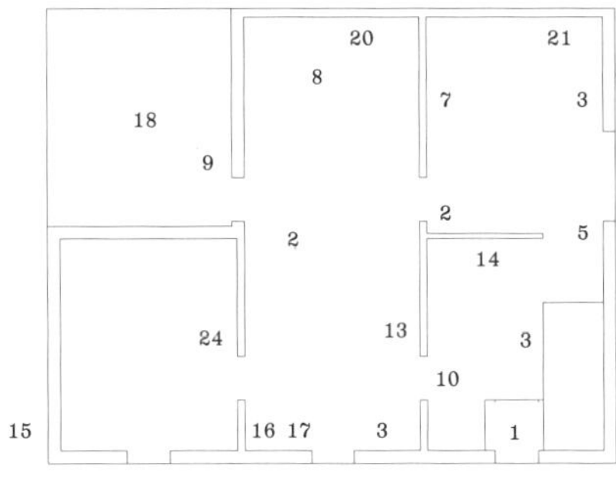


12

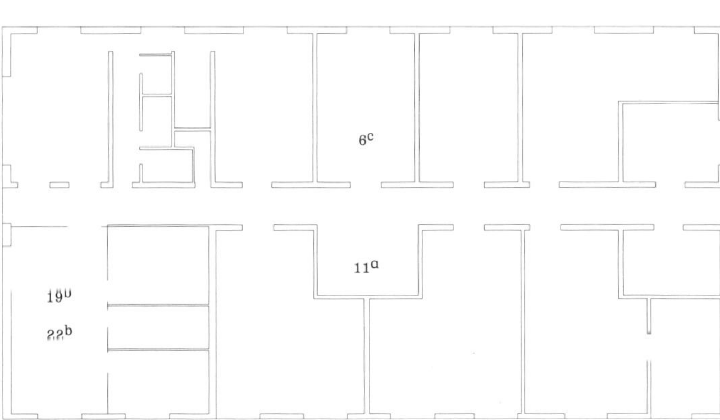

# PRELUDE

Koi Persyn

## CONVERSATIONS

Dear reader,

*The pressure of your palms* holds the publication *Fugue* that accompanies the eponymous duo exhibition by Aaron Amar Bhamra (°1992, AT) and Céline Mathieu (°1989, BE) at Jester in Genk, Belgium. Both fugues emerge from a polyphonous dialogue between 24 newly created works of art and an equal number of contributors—siblings, friends, colleagues, and peers. All work is dependent and relational, in the end. Within this conversation, Aaron Amar Bhamra interweaves his background in architecture and music, using materials from personal and social archives to orchestrate *form*. Céline Mathieu responds by imagining new tactics to rewire finances and revalue close relationships. Both artists' practices span across various fields of cultural work, assuming the roles of writer, curator, educator, and researcher. This role conversion oozes through the pages of this publication with a textual contribution by Céline Mathieu and a series of analogue photographs by Aaron Amar Bhamra. Many *occasions*, words, sounds, and images will follow in the *form* of a musical score by Charlie Usher and essays by Eloise Sweetman and Johanna Schindler. Therefore, this prelude solely sets the *Tone* for what is to come, introducing unseen stories as primal timbres that resonate with a myriad of voices.

*Céline and Aaron changed the entrance from the right to the middle door, leading you directly into a central, luminous hall. Here, you are welcomed by half a wall (Jester), a work by Aaron that actually measures half the wall you just entered through, and indicates that perception often only tells half the story. The airy space breathes like the sound box of a music instrument, reverberating the impulses of its four side chambers. Two main motives —a basin (Bekken) and a platform (midair)—find their residence here as the first voices of the composition. Previously, the basin lingered in the building for years after it lost its function as a reservoir to cool steel after welding. The platform was left behind in the archive after it supported hundreds of prints on a safe distance from the ground. Both objects were handpicked by the artists during their first site visit and now host their work as support structures. By changing the official entrance, a new emergency exit plan had to be devised for insurance compliance. The new escape routes were designed and (re)placed by Aaron's hands as untitled. Only later did we realize that "fugue" in its literal meaning also signifies the notion of an escape.*

# CONVERSIONS

*Fugue* forms a dissonant harmony of fleeting gestures that converge in a composition of counterpoint, inversion, and echo. The title originates from the Latin *fuga* (flight) and relates to its two meanings: a polyphonic musical motif and a psychological state of dissociation. The highly coded composition of a fugue—on the one hand—sets the *Tone* with multiple voices being doubled, mirrored, and halved in an emergence of new melodic themes. Repetition is key. A fugue state—on the other hand—indicates a displacement of the mind, inflicted by a traumatic experience that causes a sudden loss of memory—how did we arrive here? Both the aural and mental dimensions of a fugue inform the exhibition and the publication. Sound and air are impermanent media that materialize here by eluding the artists' voices. Encounters between substances are temporal, whether they consume, hold, or release each other. Strayed objects are stripped of their functionality and separated from their origins, almost amnesic. In *Fugue*, the artworks are numbered in a non-(chrono)logical order, led by the (dis)associative wandering of the artists' minds. Some works are to be seen only on specific days of the week (a), while others are solely accessible to Jester's employees (b) or residents (c). Bypassing the spatial conditions and conventional circulation of your ears, eyes, and noses, the artworks ascend and descend from different angles of the architectural spaces. Transient proposals take flight to the garden, studio, and residency building, while relations, resources, thoughts, and affects circulate and temporarily rest in a state of fugue.

*A zephyr comes soaring from the 163-meter high slag heap that neighbors the exhibition space. As a reminiscence of the local mining past of Genk, this monumental man-made hill stands sentinel over the post-industrial landscape. Like tidal waves of aerial masses, currents of air descend over the historic site. They cut through the passage between new and old structures, towards the 72-meter towering mine shaft. The swallows fly low and as I imagine birds talking (1-4), their squeaking seems to stir the wild wind beneath their wings. Brown leaves leave the soil in swirls. The whirlwind collides midair with the steel landmark, causing high-pitched whistles to blare across the city, as the high volume of air attempts to breach the architectural skeleton. This larger-than-life flute echoes the fire brigade's sporadic sirens when I call Céline so she can tune in:* ".

# CONVERGENCES

"Listen carefully, for all artworks whisper of times, affinities, and seasons. Watch closely, for *Tempus fugit* (time flies), and see how dissociated objects find refuge in Genk's history. Take in the scents that doze their sculptures asleep. Hurry up, before a breath swells to a breeze that carries them *on air*—when did we arrive here?"

*At the close of the nineteenth century, the* Kneipp *sanatorium landed in Bokrijk, a district of Genk, drawn by the abundance of clean—and, therefore, healthy— air. At this sanctuary, lung patients would reside to cure their tuberculosis and other respiratory ailments through hydro-, balneo-, and aërotherapy. Simultaneously, the region of Genk became a renowned* station d'artistes— *a beloved haven for painters, scientists, and writers—that flourished with the same fresh air that nourished its natural landscape. The latter fled when the mining industry of coal extraction irreversibly scarred the landscape. Oxygen was sparse in this vast, 850-meter deep network of tunnels, while its fabricators often suffered from dust lungs and other pulmonary diseases. Air carries the sound of many voices and the weight of many histories: on the one hand healing through purity and presence, on the other hand, harmful through pollution and absence. Air quality and health remain, therefore, inseparable and indispensable to all life, then and now.*

Enjoy the flight of *former tulip and string.*

# EXHIBITION TEXT

Céline Mathieu

We scrambled up the order of the numbers on the floor plan, just like we changed the entry door to the kunsthal, just like we put artworks in all adjacent buildings, too—from the office desks, to the garden, to the hallway, to one of the studios, and to the residency house, *Fugue* continues.

In this duo exhibition by Aaron Amar Bhamra and Céline Mathieu, one may encounter feelings of elusiveness and dissociation, of flight-like curves and of different musical lines finding harmony mid-sentence. Yet, pressing back on all-too-thin-ness, Aaron drew architectural floor plans and Céline wrote this very text that also exists as an audio guide. Both artists share a love for details, titles, and material lists; a key to the reading of both their practices.

Collected every autumn by Aaron and his family, a batch of walnuts is exhibited the year that follows. As the title suggests—an "occasion" to re-root personally. A nut is irreversibly open or closed. When cracking it to know what is inside, its form is broken, creating a new form, and there is no moment to reconfigure the shell once it is cracked. Many works of Aaron re-appear, self-refer, and construct a sort of inner logic or inner poetic ABAB structure between different exhibitions. The nuts, for one, were previously used to denote time, walnuts from 2020, 2021, and 2022 each with their own traits. As they are often exhibited, dried after the autumn's harvest, they have paused, and represent the past. In brief, walnuts lay open, half shells on the floor, what looks like a piece of folded fabric is actually—for those attentive enough to read the material list—half a wall.

I, Céline, moved this dysfunctional sink that I found in the studio building hallway of Jester, to the exhibition space, where it now becomes sculptural. It reveals in its basin my friend Joëlle's silk shirt, soaking in coconut oil. She told me about feeding the silk with coconut oil last summer, to the mention of which I shivered, and she said: "Exactly. It sounds like a work of yours." I'm showing a paper skirt, made while playing; cut in strips and drawn on by my friend Andrea and her two-and-a-half-year-old. It then hung on the wall of their studio, where I saw it almost every day, and I kept thinking of how I could own it without owning it. So, I asked her if I could present it as a work, something she didn't intend as such. Same with the calendar she drew following the form of what time looks like in her mind, a snaking curved shape. I asked her to draw one for me without mentioning the months and I name her in the material list as a maker. For each of these appropriated, unintended works, I ask the person what compensation they see fit; in general,

or in case of sale. From this conversation on value and worth, I agree
with what they propose our respective parts of the work are worth.

A kite lays dormant, for which two modular parts are made to measure.
The kite is a work Aaron has been making variations on for years;
this is the third variation of this piece. First shown in a church, the kite
there had three or four components. The entire structure of a kite
was cast in aluminum, and his sister made the "garments" for it. This
work plays with the different layers of skin; of object, of subject, and
of architecture. In the different iterations, the kite and its handles are
always disconnected. In the second iteration, Aaron showed more of
a skeleton, presenting the kite in the foyer and its handles in the exhibition space. The kite at Jester has no handles; someone would use it
with their body in the sky—the kite and the subject stand in a one-to-one
relation. The structuring components of the wings are excerpted and
lay displayed, leaving behind a sleep-like kite.

The ventilator sound I recorded inside the institution is now playing
outside, in the little courtyard. My friend Ginevra hums along to Jester's
ventilator sound. She is mimicking a YouTube video called *Girl harmonising with fan*. When I told her I'd never seen it, she shouted in dis-
belief, so I commissioned her in turn to, indeed, harmonise with the
fan for me. The sound is hypnotising, has something of a pipe doing
its thing, or a hum you'd pick up from a factory, finding yourself walking past, alone, surprised by having ended up—here.
  On the ground of the courtyard lay the lower part of my cropped
jacket and a garment by textile chemist Rosie Broadhead. Made up
of 75% viscose, 20% algae, and 5% elastane; the viscose is derived from
the cellulose of eucalyptus trees in this case, but is chemically processed
to create the yarn. The Tic Tac mints on top are minty fresh, and will
sugar coat and chemically engage with the garments over time. Mint-
eucalyptus is one of the classic scents in the skin products line of Kneipp,
who formerly erected a sanatorium here in Bokrijk, close to Jester.
I was also interested in eucalyptus trees being used, as they grow so fast;
yet meanwhile present a considerable threat, being one of the most
flammable trees, leading to increased wildfires.

Aaron's duo of chairs holds an aluminum cast of the plate and the strips
of architecture foam that are the remnants of carving a perfect seat cover
for the Thonet 209. Gifted to Aaron by his former professor and his
wife, the Thonet chairs iconically bend the wood in three directions.
A form is cast in bronze, holding a shape, and is presented in a cardboard

box. Daylight and exhibition light reflect in his empty metal light shades, which were used in the first three exhibitions of *Laurenz* between 2020 and 2021 in Vienna.

I was inspired by Genk's history of being a place people came to for rest and fresh air, with a famous Kneipp sanatorium erected here in Bokrijk. That's one history lesser known, compared to what came after; lives lived and dusted in the mines. The doctor who discovered the dust lung lives next-door here.

A frame shows four photographs I found of the Kneipp sanatorium director's house. Both text and images come from the Flemish inventory of architectural heritage online. I like how the photographs taken in 2017 by Charlotte Fexer, and a description aiming to convey rich histories of decay, can become an artwork for their evocative properties. Telling in ways of money, health, and thick layers of reality and estates. The text describes how the building was planted in front of a very long, narrow plot on the north side of Hasseltweg. That the owner at the time was Eugenius Josephus Armandus Simons, a notary in Liège. That it used to be this man's hunting house, when the woods were still around to cater. The text speaks of owners changing; of how it was purchased to become the house of Kneipp, the director of Belgium's first sanatorium—where hydro- and balneotherapy were used to cure tuberculosis. It mentions in the same tone the architectural elements and adjustments, like the way the neo-classical elements faded and the interior, too, and that the interior was caught in flames in the end. It says it is now used for catering. I asked my friend Matt Hinkley to design it. The original dry description's elements evoke images possibly borrowed from movies. The images seem enchanted by dread and hints of horror.

A paper column stands as if it has stripped the absent whiteness of the space's wall, condensing it into an object. The paper roll's cut-outs create patterns of light. These cut-outs match the shapes that Aaron displayed at Kevin Space in Vienna. The shapes then were inspired by an unfolded pastry box with four flaps that resemble tulip petals. Aaron assigned each petal to a different voice *(1st soprano, 2nd soprano, 1st alto, 2nd alto)*, exploring how these four voices learn to harmonise with one another during rehearsal.

A collaborative edition stays in the storage. Depicting the change of entries, a fire escape plan becomes part of the exhibition. Do read the material lists and the titles, if you want to see what you're looking at:

"*untitled, 2025, 369 m2, print on paper, (publicly accessible areas of Jester–Kunsthal, Genk).*" While the mandatory infrastructural elements in an exhibition space often bother people, Aaron appropriates the fire escape plans both for their materiality and for the way they simply depict space. A fire exit plan shows a point of where you stand in the space, making you aware of your location within an exhibition context; within an architecture. The exit plans also work as a guideline to empty the space: they tell you how to exit, in other words how to remove the subject from the architectural context. The work's dimensions account for all publicly accessible square meters of the kunsthal.

Speaking of access, closing the original entry with a veneer wall, I made a little scented cabin. In it hangs the cut paper skirt my friend cut and drew with her daughter. The exhibition guard regularly sprays Molecule n°1, a pheromone-enhancing perfume, on the veneer.

There are glasses of beer with raw egg yolks in them, with a shot of whiskey on the side, which is what miners used to have for breakfast, a formerly existing work of mine–Céline's–fitting into Genk's historical context. Outside, between the kunsthal and the residency house, Aaron's *The pressure of your palms* refers to the system used in Belvedere in Vienna to separate the places for walking and the place where flowers sleep and grow. A moment of defining where to be and not– the pressure of your palms. The soundscape of birds singing becomes part of the work. On the kunsthal's façade, my thread connects the water pipe to the floor preventing dripping sounds–inspired by a gesture by T.B.

Aaron's bird series is captured all the same, but with a slight turn of the head, and is printed on green and white left-behind paper. They stay in the four respective bedrooms of the residents, and will land in this publication, too, but merely live in the mind's eye of the exhibition visitor. Similarly, there are Aaron's paperweights on the office desks at Jester. Left behind on the desk of Jester's team, the paperweights Aaron uses at home have now come here. This, he said, leaves him time and creates the need to make or find two new paperweights during the time of the exhibition. One of them was found in Brussels while out on a trip with the curator Koi and Céline. The other one looks like a gothic church bundle column and usually lives atop a pile of floor plans at his house. At the office of Jester, they are here for daily use, for the team and the documentation only. Same for a note of mine that is copied on *Fugue*'s flyers by others. In one of the studios, Aaron's projection is shown; it's an image of a red tissue holding its form, whilst its surroundings keep moving. It will be on display until the arrival of the next resident. There is a work by Aaron on the cars of the curator and assistant curator titled *anti-collision oiseaux*. In Jester's hallway, there is a library of what is left of my books after years of travel. They are displayed on plexi shelves with a woodworker's first exercise— a set of Max Bill stools, both a seat, step, and carrying device. The stools, designed with Jan Omer Fack, were crafted by Stef Renard, the entire piece was produced and financed by Jester. Interested in circulating material and funds, *The Library* was first exhibited at a small art space in Brussels called celador before coming here, where it will stay for the duration of this exhibition and beyond it as a permanent work, swapping my personal books, with Jester's growing archive. The latter two works are visible only during office hours on Wednesdays and Thursdays.

The "air" of this exhibition is possibly in vein of a video of a plastic bag that seems to be dancing to Bach. A seemingly effortless choreography emerges, shaped by many factors and timings—not least the person aiming the camera. Here, the assistance of a title and listed materials helps hold this shape, at this moment, from this angle.

# FUGUE
piano / recordings

$\quad \bigl. \bigr. = 60$

Charlie Usher

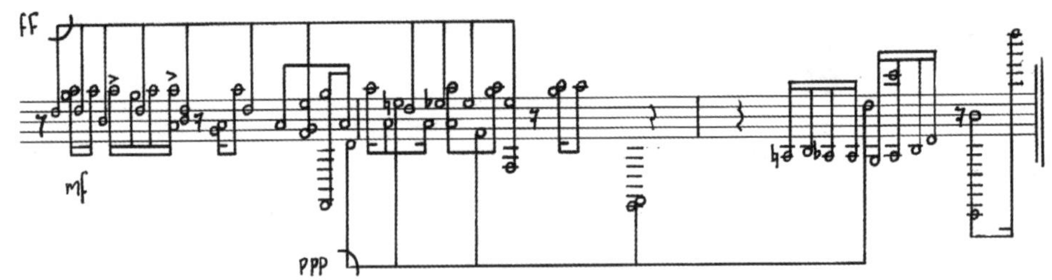

ff
mf
ppp


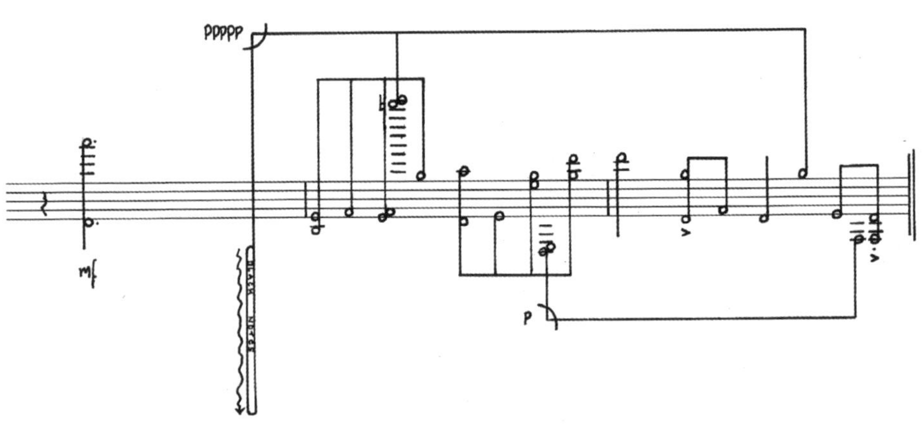

pppp
mf
p


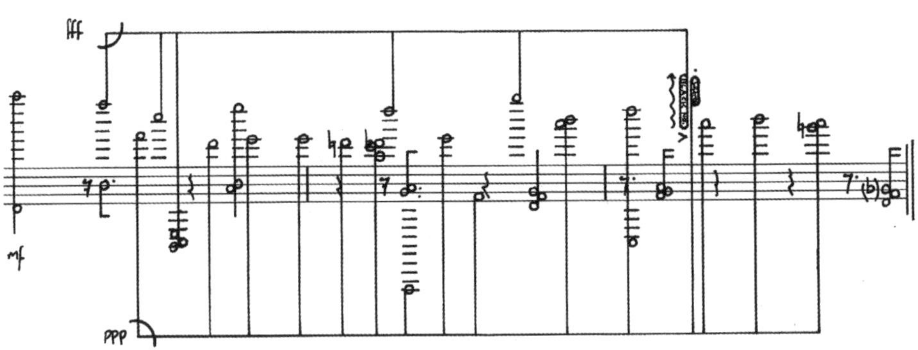

fff
mf
ppp

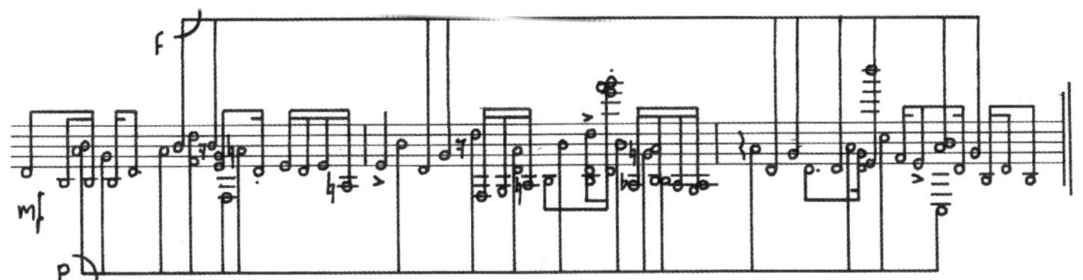

Each section:

treble clef

4/4

key signature: five flats

♩= 60 is average tempo; speed up and slow down
Dynamics apply to all notes from same voice / beam
Maximum contrast between dynamics for maximum depth of field
Heavy sustain pedal smears and is always held between sections
Minimum 30" between sections

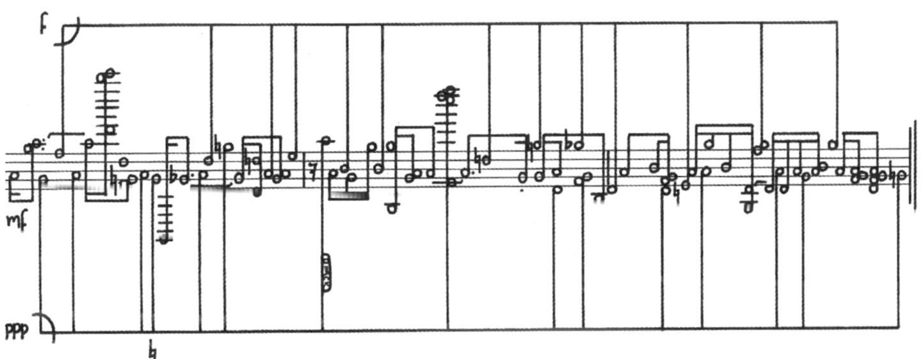

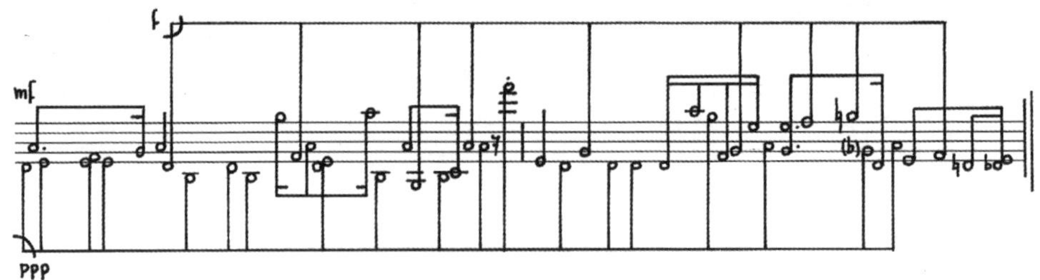

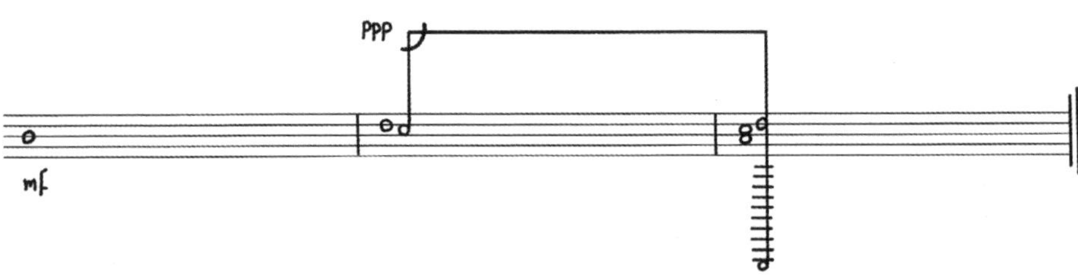

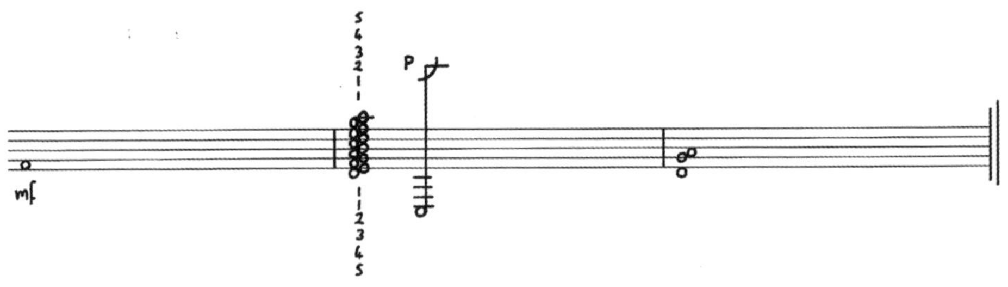

# HISTORY IS IN EVERYTHING,
# OR ECHO RECALLS HERSELF

Eloise Sweetman

Standing outside in the courtyard I watch the wings of a wind turbine swing around and out of view. A hill–an important place so I am told– obscures most of the sky and its vanes.

Crouching down, I look at borrowed fabric (18) amongst the grasses and weeds. The white garment appears to have white fuzzy mold growing on it. Looking longer, I see that it is a thin crust of almost thawed snow. The sun is warm, and the last bit of ice dissolves the tic tac on the black textile, leaving an unwelcome chalky residue.

I am breathing in. I am breathing out.


Name one thing you can smell: minty-eucalyptus.
Name one thing you can touch: the aged rough wool of my second-hand jacket.


Rocking on my heels, I return my gaze to the borrowed view outside this place. I listen to the sound of the turbine, a low hum that I join, the kind of hum that you feel rather than vocalize. Another hum (9) joins us and then a fourth, a quartet of voices and machines. Each starts the same, but finally, we take our distinctive paths.


Is it really true that we are alone at the end?
I am breathing in. I am breathing out.


Standing up, fists reaching the sky, my wings (2) curl around me and I go back inside.


Walnuts (17) crack underfoot, collected yearly, they are broken forever. Recycled, renewed, re-remembered.

Resting my feet upon the bent wood of Le Corbusier's favorite chair (10),
I warm myself in the chunk of light pushing its way into the darkened
wood-paneled room. I am wondering how I can get back on track.


At least let me tell you this:
All the artworks are more than what you see now, they extend time
and space beyond what you read. Perhaps our experience will be a
marker of, and a reference in, the future. Like a love song that we once
sang to each other will be sung by someone else. A melody hummed
by someone who does not know that this was about us, here, reading
this together.

Time travel is assured.
Memory, they say, is reincarnation.

But still, my heart aches knowing the song will be better if we take
different directions.


Justice is out of reach.


Walnuts crack underfoot (17).


I am sure the two young women on their way home from the club called
me mother.
Not daring to turn around, I watch fat pink clouds blow away. The sky
is brilliant, and they hug goodbye. I fold back up the white fabric,
the half-size of a door that they troubled at trying to get my attention.
They both leave. One walks home, and the other watches the water
from her seat, as it carries her home.


There is still so much to tell you, like about the doors that left a jar and
tulips taped to a disused sink and silk feeding on coconut oil (8), pro-
jected water reflected in another room (6c & 7), and decal birds on the
cars of Karel and Koi (23a).

There are spaces within spaces like an old peach box (7) living its new
life as an artwork, a carrier: watery (6c) and reflected. Spaces within
spaces like a foot inside a tailored sock by a loving sister (2) or a paper
skirt carefully cut to size by a mother and her proud daughter (1).

History is in everything; like time it fills space.
Spaces within spaces within spaces.
Valued.



The young men behind me speak excitedly about Amazing Race and
the economy in a cloud of blackberry cough drops. A kind lady sprays
Molecule No. 1, as I come around the corner.

"Of course, you can come in,"
she tells me,
"I perfumed the room just for you" (1).


Embarrassed and impressed, I wait for her to leave, as I do the fingers
of borrowed orange light caress the white underbelly of the day. I press
4c on my audio guide and listen to Céline as she tells me about artworks whose audiences are the ones who are there to sleep (4c). I press
22b and hear about artworks that have been given new homes (22b).

These numbers are out of sync.
Not waiting for their ordered turns, they transform the fugue into a
round.
My son and I sing about how our life is



I wave to Aaron, and we walk to Céline and Koi.

Us four talk a little,
Smokey breath mingles in the breeze.



    Walnut crack underfoot (17).

Worried that I said the wrong thing, I walk alongside dried flowers
threaded through outsized eyelets staked into the ground (12).
The collection borders winter-bleached gardens, but sure enough,
already weeks early, the bright yellow petals of the daffodil catch
my eye.

Echo recalls herself back to me. I think of the Greek myth about the
chatty cheerful nymph who watches the man she loves kiss his watery
reflection until he wastes away.
"Farewell" is the final word that she speaks before turning into a
stoney cave.

Another echo,
spaces across spaces.
Absence tells of its presence.


I am breathing in. I am breathing out.


Time lingers and fills the room like perfume (1).

# BROKEN RECORD

Johanna Schindler

In a conversation, how do you encounter each other       in the same space

*Without architecture—understood as a space designed by someone—there is no sound. Without air, water or materials such as glass and concrete, there is no transmission and reflection of sound waves. Their meeting is exciting because it is often impossible to distinguish between them: Is it the space that determines a sound? Or is it the sound that defines a space and its dimensions?* (Jan St. Werner, 2021)

and when you meet each other, how do you refer to the form of the process of the progress of the change over time of the seasons of the different states of the response of the iteration of the variation of the composition of the dissolution of the diffusion of the reassembling of the recollection of the joint of the fixation of the refusal of the reason of the undefined of the indefinite of the long gone of the in-between       when what you're referring to is by no means new to you, since you've looked at it from so many different angles over and over and over again and turned it around and repeated the argument in your head and added a voice that repeated the argument with a counterpoint in your head and added a voice that repeated another argument echoing in your head which you had improvised on and experimented with and bent in every direction so really, you've heard it all before and can argue every side and you know, of course, that when concepts travel through discourses, spaces, bodies, languages by being renegotiated, clarified, translated in every encounter really, they take on different meanings, sounds, values, effects which might be new to someone present and that someone might even be you because your understanding of it might be different after all or change yet again when while vocalizing what you recently thought you realize what you've said, understanding it only now really
listening to the time that has passed between the first inscription and the ways you are finding now to make sense of it, using words that sit in your mouth comfortably maybe, when you talk about a personal occasion you hold dearly in your heart, that are scattered and shattered mostly, when you return to a story weighing on your heart so heavily that you can hardly contain it yet need to crush it into pieces to be bearable and breathable, or thick and sticky, when you revisit the same term, the same form, the same subjectobject yet again to hold it tight while it holds you tight and you try to rid yourself of it       *Knock knock!*


(Sarah Ahmed, 2022)

*To knock on the door is to turn up, to keep turning up, to find new forms of expression. We knock on the door not to demand entry but to cause a disturbance, to disturb the spirits who linger here because of the violence that has not been dealt with . . . . To turn up is to turn up for each other saying not "knock, knock, who is there?" but "knock, knock, we are here."* (Sara Ahmed, 2022)

because after looking for its parts in private, public, and personal archives, in shelves and shells of albums and reels and spools and cylinders and bolts and rolls and scrolls and everything that spins like a siren, *rotating slowly at first, so that you were not able to hear the air vibrating* (Hermann von Helmholtz, 1971) but sensed it anyways, faster and faster then, with the sensation becoming audible and you humming along affirmatively because you knew you were onto something, and even faster still, *taking up all the weak and the strong signals* (Eyal Weizman, 2022) to follow or not follow, and you create files and folders and lists and indexes and schedules and budgets and plans and you go through photos and maps and catalog entries and copies of documents and transcriptions of copies including your great-grandmother's handwritten notes about her time on the mission for the Moravian church which simply stop with your grandmother's birth even though her life continued well after that and which your great-cousin or some relative along those lines transcribed with a typewriter and scanned and emailed to their sibling who saved them on a USB-stick and mailed them to you with a letter to which you replied with a CD you bought in the web shop of a museum that stores ethnomusicological recordings including those your great-uncle made on missions in former German East Africa in the 1930s with a recording device whose stylus put the sound of indigenous people's singing and instrumental play down in invisibly trembling lines onto 45 wax cylinders which have last been played for digitization and since then been still for conservational reasons, and you travel to the Moravian church's boarding school your grandmother and approximately 2000 kids went to between 1790 and 1942 and meet one of the archivists of the protestant community's village who sent you scans of the institution's register of entry and exit dates and gives you a tour through the hallway and dining room and the girls' dormitory underneath the roof of the Sisters' house which is in need of renovation and on the EU Commission's list of most endangered cultural heritage sites 2023 and around the square and explains that the doctor's cabinet used to be a pharmacy used to be a Kolonialwarenladen and when you go into the archive and take in the smell of the old paper you think,

Somehow this is like digging up someone's grave, not in the death-drive kind of way but in the curious kind of way to understand the relation between body and space, and you're not quite sure whether that someone is present and whether it's you, going deeper and deeper, and depending on the soil composition you might find humid earth or soft sand and spores and roots and rubble and dusty particles and you're not quite sure what it is that you're inhaling, in any case that's what you do when you're autobioethnographicosoundmediasociopsychotheoreticoknowledgehistorically trying to show that bodies and buildings and soil and air carry voices, knowledges, and histories through time and space no matter how often they change ownership or are inhabited or destroyed because they'll be rebuilt and reused and reclaimed, which is still new and hard to grasp and denied by some present even though you feel like the stylus and the cylinder, in their fairytale-like conjunction, are proving the point so obviously that it's almost sarcastic, and then again your subjectobject is so much more ephemeral, and knowing that much gets lost in translation and transfer and conversion, faster still faster, and that material withers or dries or dissolves, still faster, and while what has been saidheardsensed through all of these records and their residues and gaps is slowly moving from your ear and nose and arm hairs to form wrinkles on your forehead or to tense your neck muscles or to cramp your stomach, reaching into your heart or causing you to fidget about, your eyes are searching for a direction and your breath externalizes what has been grasped, passing it on, allowing it to sag, and absorbs what has not yet been understood although where there is smoke

  *Faster and faster I should run* (Janelle Monáe, 2010)  your body just  leaves  you


*Smell is elusive. Its effects surprise us. We don't know how to put much about smell into words, even when our reactions are strong and certain. Humans breathe and smell in the same intake of air, and describing smell seems almost as difficult as describing air. But smell, unlike air, is a sign of the presence of another, to which we are already responding. Response always takes us somewhere new; we are not quite ourselves any more—or at least the selves we were, but rather ourselves in encounter with another. Encounters are, by their nature, indeterminate; we are unpredictably transformed. Might smell, in its confusing mix of elusiveness and certainty, be a useful guide to the indeterminacy of encounter?* (Anna Tsing, 2015)

and again, with no or only little access to language, to your memory,
to your feelings, your sense of time, without knowing whether what
has been saidheardsensed was real or fiction and whether there was
something you missed out on, some sort of shift in a connecting, sur-
rounding, elusive element like air, a tone, some clue, a word, a contra-
diction, you being human, all of that or something completely different      you're kind of activated and exhausted and confused and dizzy
and frustrated and unsure and lost and determined and dislocated
and present at the same time, because how on earth are you supposed
to recollect and make sense of this without any notes which you never
bothered taking because, It's all in your head, so you try to *Hold your
own / When everything is fluid / and when nothing can be known with any
certainty / Hold your own / Hold it 'til you feel it there / As dark, and dense,
and wet as earth / As vast, and bright, and sweet as air* (Kae Tempest,
2014) and you slowly take a step back, and one more, and one more
      and then you start to remember that the other day, you found a
space in which your voice could stay clear, outward facing and soft, and
that you managed to maintain that space for quite a while, hesitatingly
at first, aware of the fragility of that moment when trying to hold on
to a sound—or shape, for that matter—can lead to retaining the breath
and tightening up the throat and pulling backwards and [take a chok-
ing inhale], then, with every repetition, you savored the sounds formed
between your upper lip, nose, and the front part of your palate, a space
you had been trying to access for a long time, which is why to retain
the body memory of that space like a bookmark had been important
to you, since only then you could be sure that you'd be able, eventu-
ally, not always, not every time, to reactivate the sensation that partic-
ular soundspace created in yourself: ease and glowing softness, love
with which, once there, right up front, you were able to add timbre and
shades to the tones, leaning in, with open ears and eyes to what was
going on and sharing it with listeners at the same time, What a light
and somehow rare place to be in, you thought, to be singinglistening
clearly and softly with ease in connection with the surroundings, and
*birds flying high, you know how I feel* (Nina Simone, 1965)


*Sound doesn't imply an ideal observational position. We cannot claim
that the sound of an instrument is an object with sharply drawn con-
tours, which from a certain perspective becomes ideally graspable in its
shape, statement and purpose, and which presents itself as an absolute.
On the contrary, sound is incompleteness. It is the essence of the porous,
the corrupt, the inversion of everything solid. As soon as sound appears,*

and you remind yourself that singing often takes speaking as a start-
ing point, to improve clarity of the text and—in your case—to move
the voice from the throat to the fore, projecting outwards, into an
imagined space, with a clear intention, and while listeningsinging on
that other day you thought to yourself, What a beautiful space this
would be to navigate conflict or hold a conversation in      and then
you take another step back, and one more, and let the whole of it rest,
or simmer, as it were, ferment, depending on the ingredients, hiber-
nate, for those who prefer to lie dormant like *Orlando* (Virginia Woolf,
1928), at peace in any case, with no involvement from your end nor
anybody who contributed so far, leaving time and space to transition,
and when the time is right, And trust me, you'll know, you'll listen
to it another time, look at it again, smell the odors and imagine the flavors
it may have developed over time, and maybe a container will have
cracked and will seem to be ruined and you'll rhetorically ask Ursula
(Ursula K. Le Guin, 1986), What's that supposed to mean for the
speculative part of my endeavor, and you'll already know the reply, Well,
you could think of it as a form you might refer to as the form of the
process of the progress of the change over time of the seasons . . .

1   Ahmed, Sara. 2022. "Feminist Ears." *feminstkilljoys* blog, June 1. Available online: https://feministkilljoys.com/2022/06/01/feminist-ears/.

*   Baraitser, Lisa. 2017. *Enduring Time*. London: Bloomsbury.

*   Binnie, Imogen. 2022 [2013]. *Nevada*. London, New York: Picacord.

2   Le Guin, Ursula K. 2019 [1986]. *The Carrier Bag Theory of Fiction*. Ignota Books.

*   Machado, Carmen Maria. 2018. "Mary When You Follow Her." *Virginia Quarterly Review*, Summer, pp. 128–130.

*   McKittrick, Katherine. 2021. *Dear Science and Other Stories*. Durham: Duke University Press.

3   Monáe, Janelle. *Faster*, from *The ArchAndroid* album, released in 2010.

4   Simone, Nina. *Feeling Good*, from the *I Put a Spell on You* album, recorded in 1965.

5   St. Werner, Jan. 2021. "Beyond the Sweet Spot. Questions About Sound, Distance, and the People in Between." In: *The Sound of Distance. New Conceptions of Music, Space, and Architecture*, program booklet Haus der Kulturen der Welt, ed. by Arno Raffainer, here pp. 10–11. Available online: https://archiv.hkw.de/media/en/texte/pdf/2021_1/programm_2021/the_sound_of_distance_begleitheft.pdf.

6   Tempest, Kae. 2014. *Hold Your Own*. London: Picador.

7   Tsing, Anna. 2015. *The Mushroom at the End of the World*. Princeton and Oxford: Oxford University Press, here p. 46.

8   von Helmholtz, Hermann. 1971. „Über die physiologischen Ursachen der musikalischen Harmonie." Lecture, available online: https://www.projekt-gutenberg.org/helmholt/raumkraf/chap007.html.

9   Weizman, Eyal. 2022. "Open Verification." In: *The New Institution*, ed. by Bern Scherer, publication series The New Alphabet #25, Leipzig: Spector Books, pp. 68–80.

10  Woolf, Virginia. 2016 [1928]. *Orlando: A Biography*. London: Penguin.



Thank you A., A., A., A., C., E., E., I., L., K., K., K., S. for your invitation to write this text, our exchanges, for working with me and my voice, and for pushing me to go further.

12.02.2025

Aaron Amar Bhamra

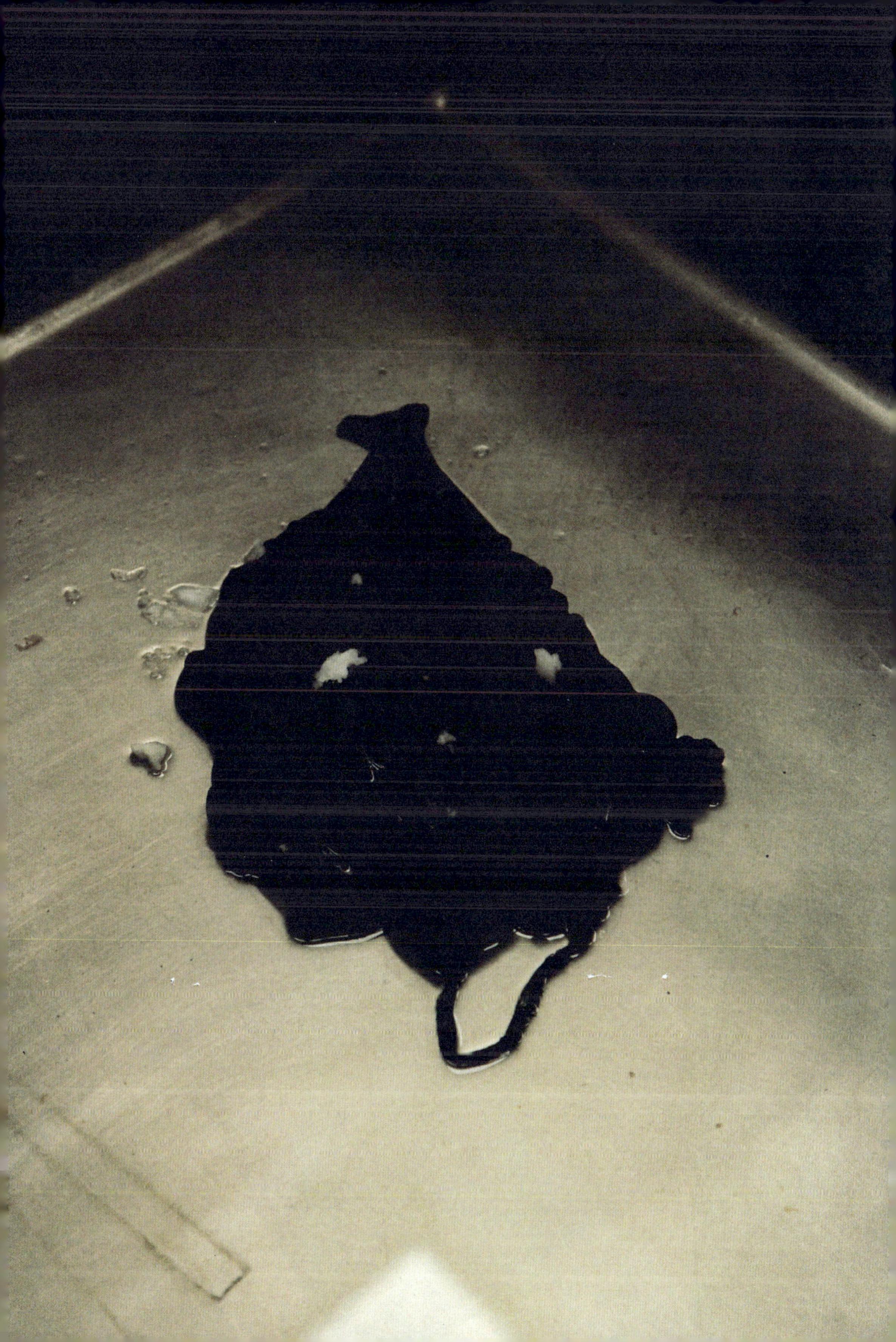

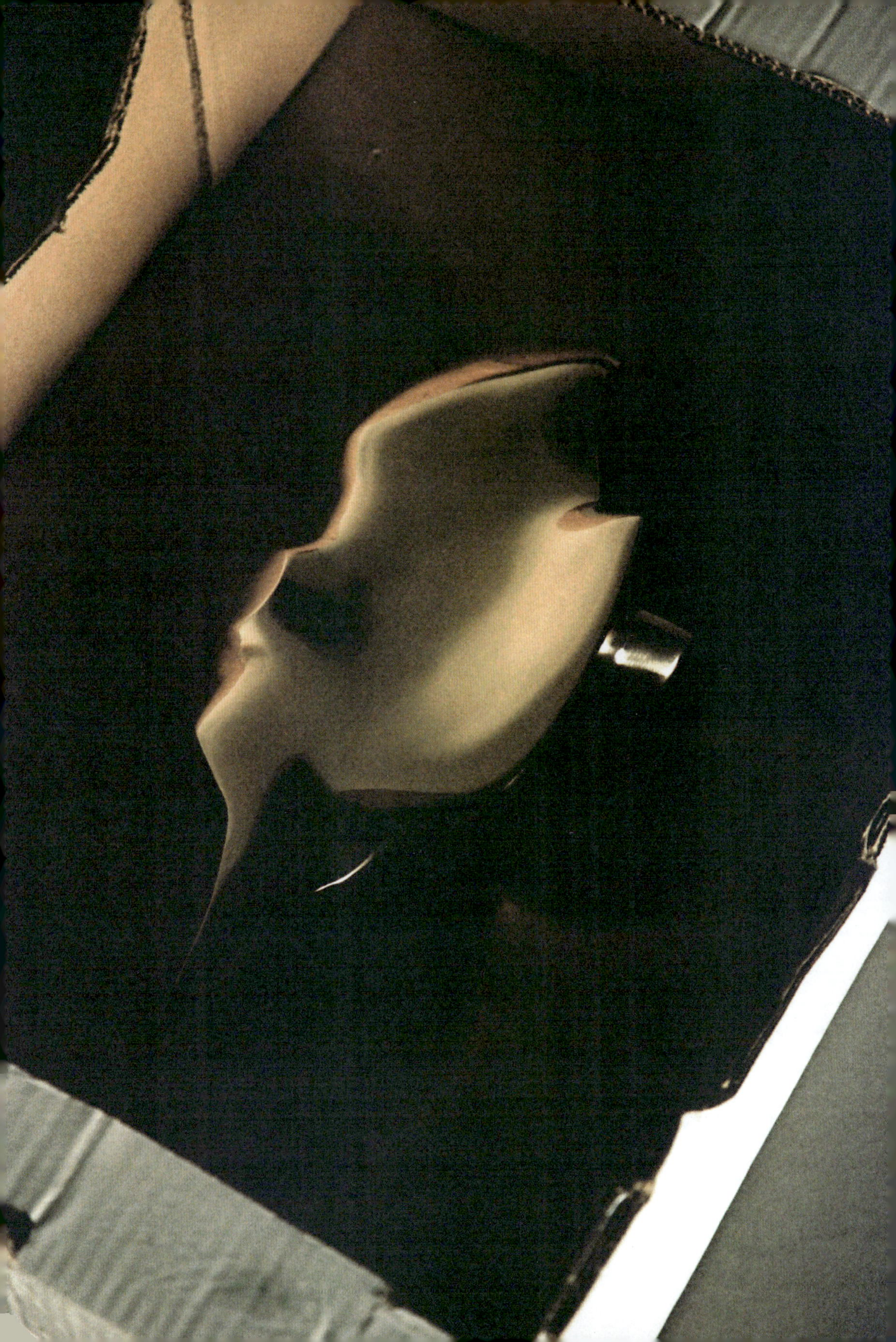

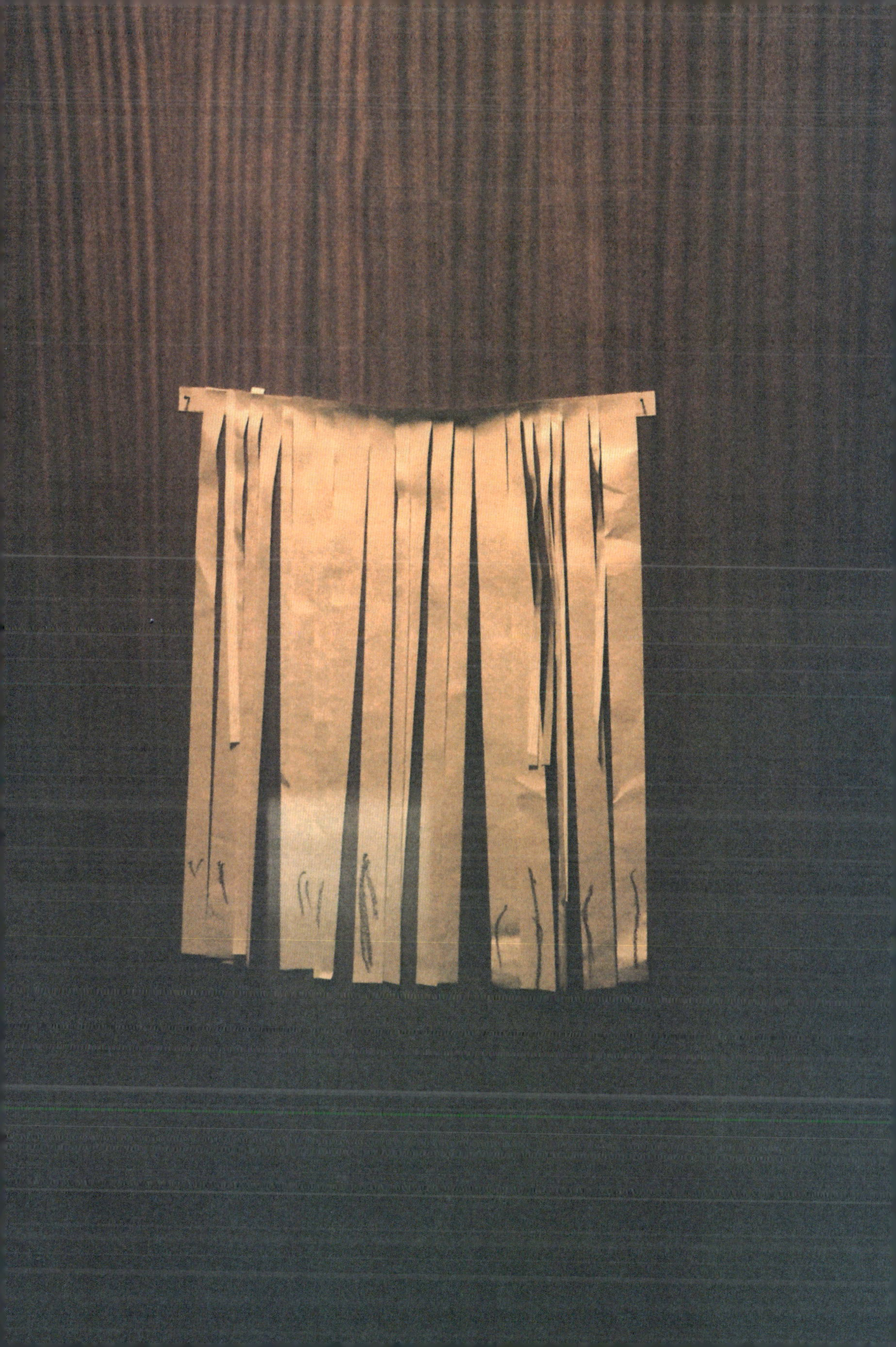

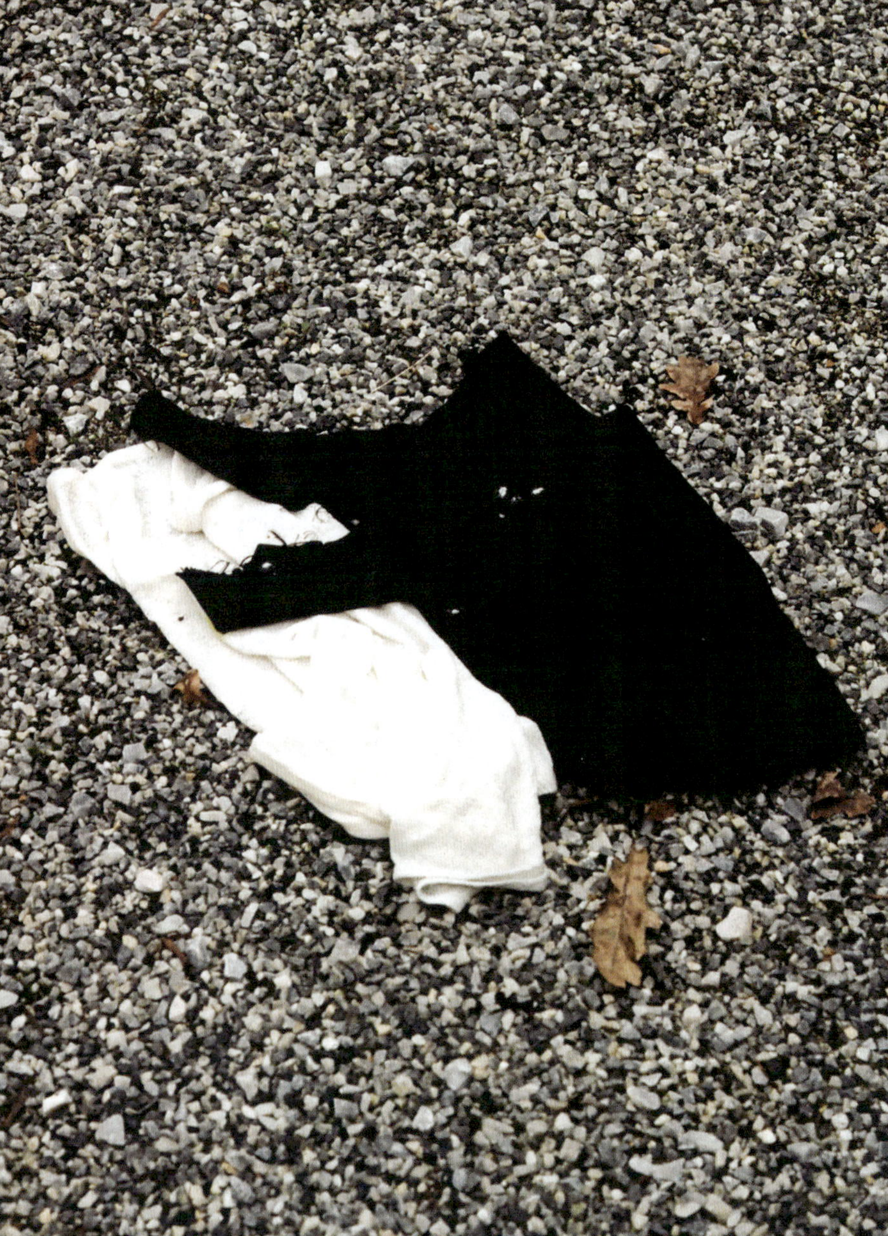

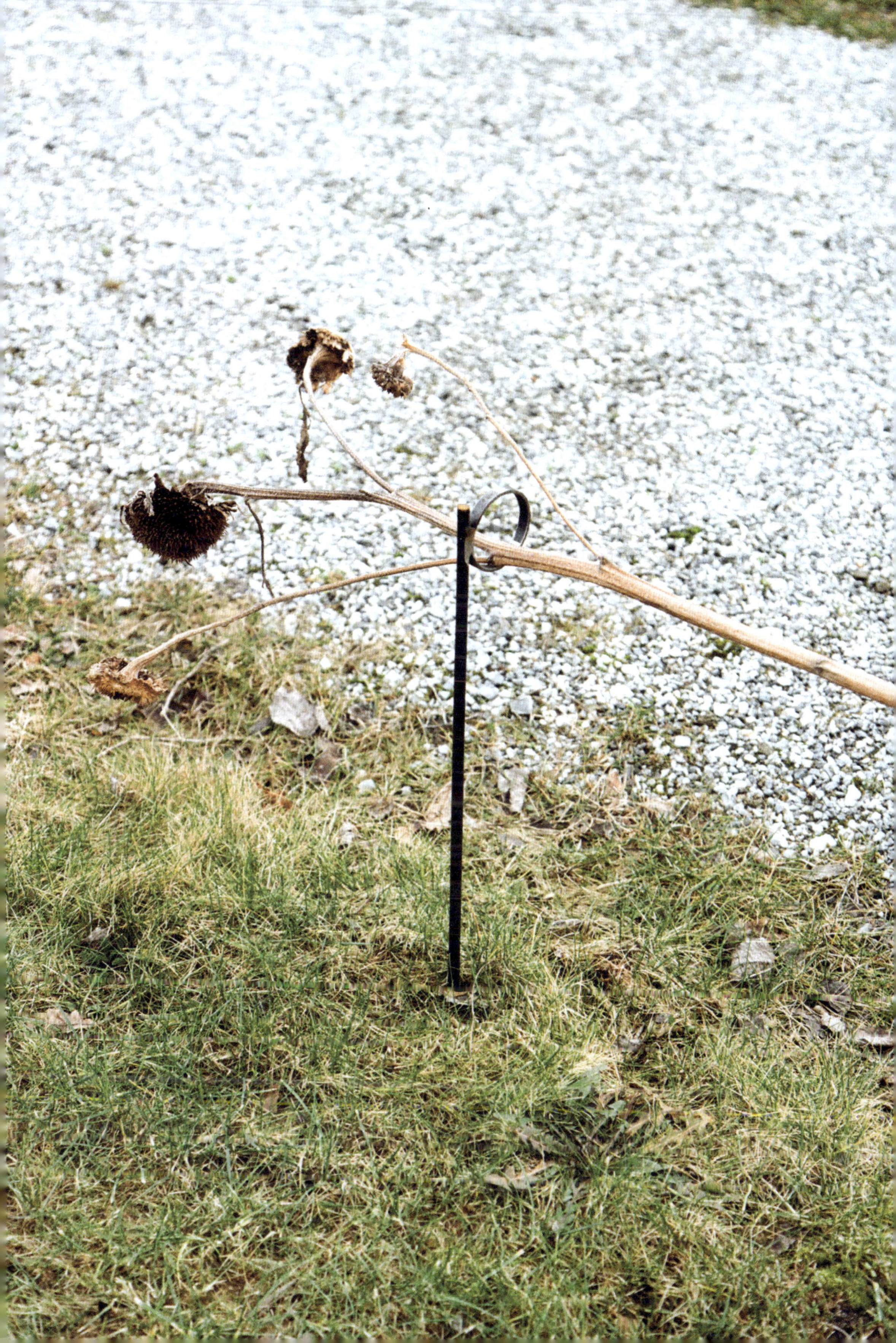

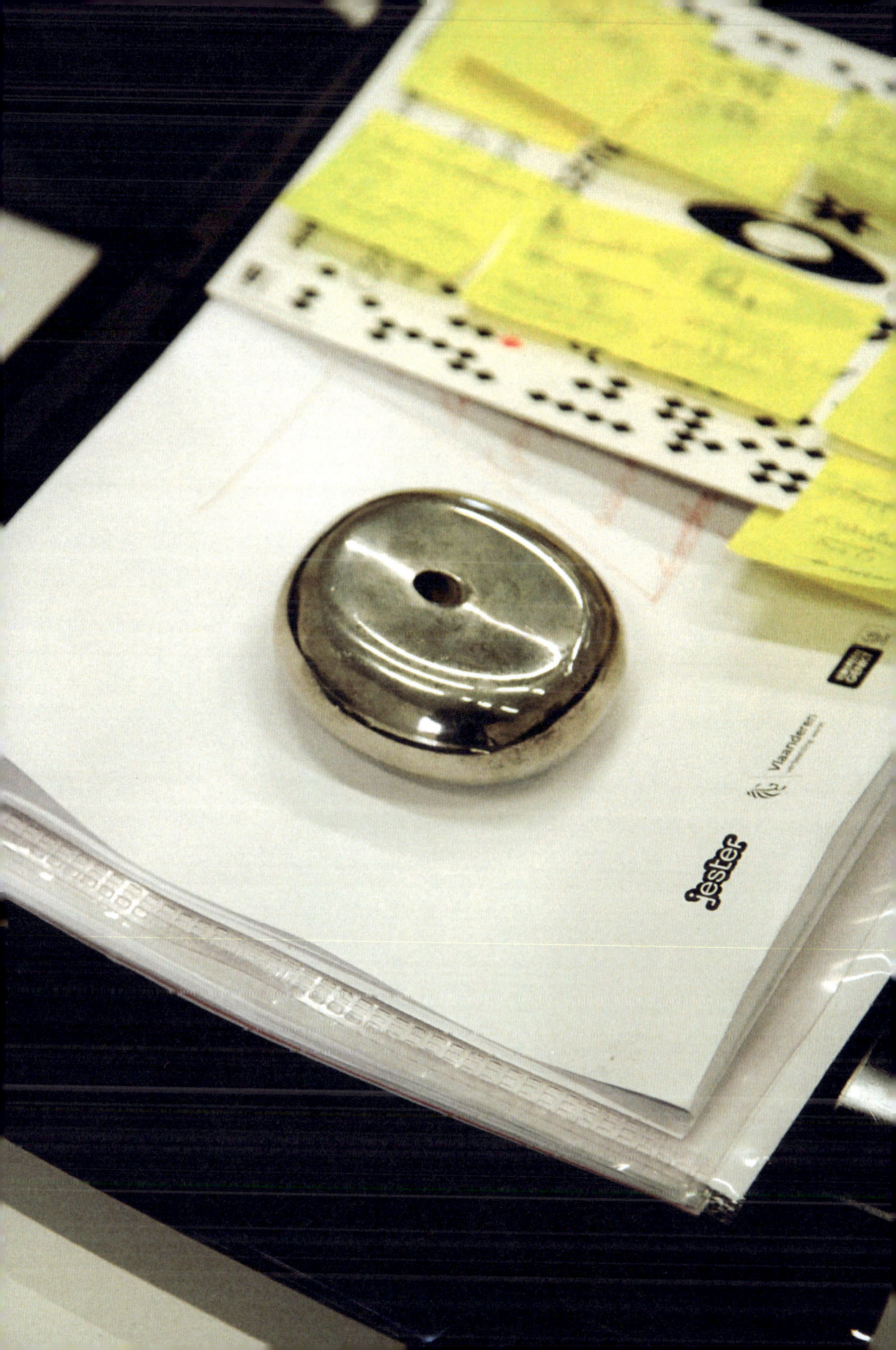
Jester
vlaanderen

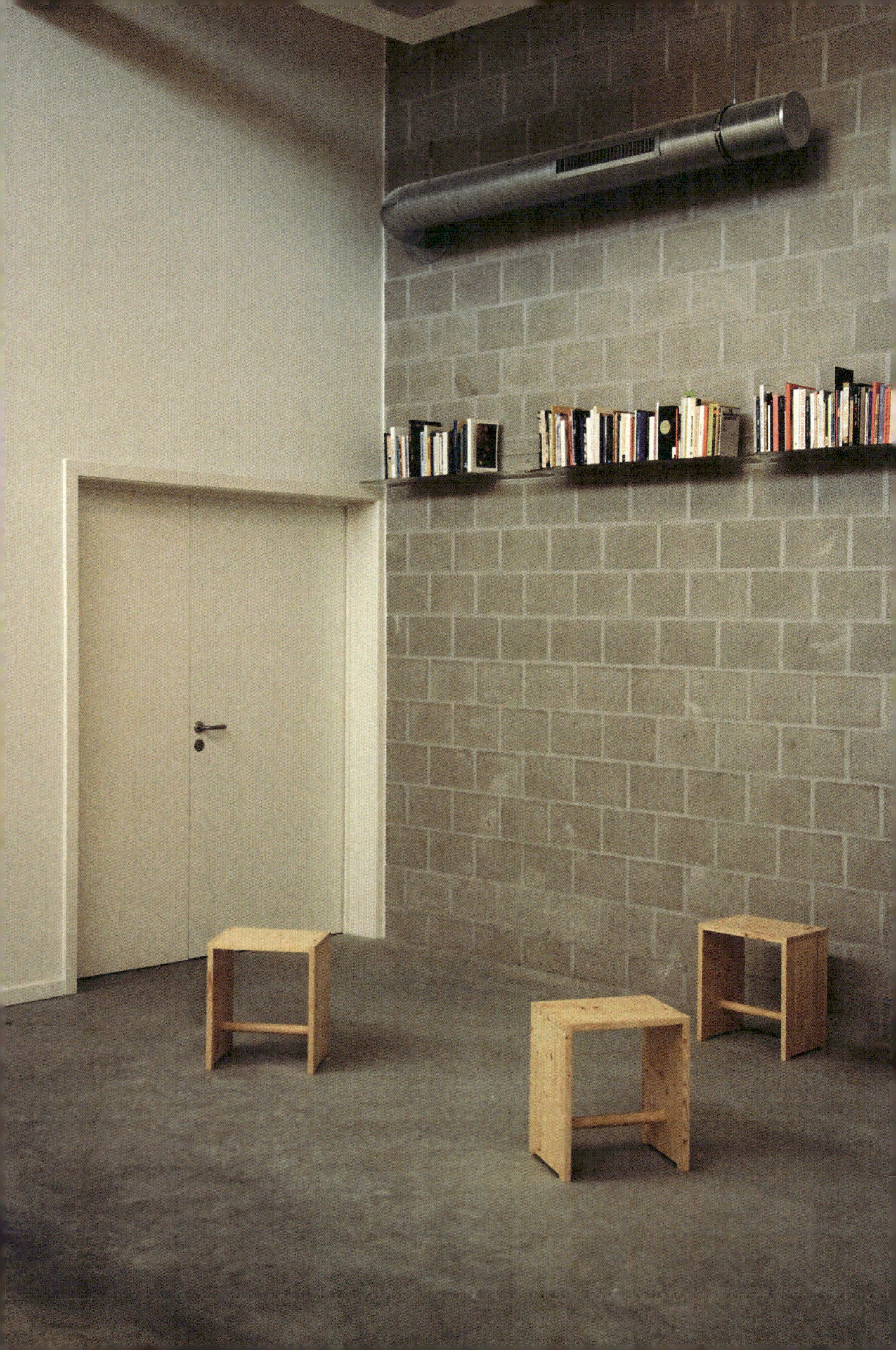

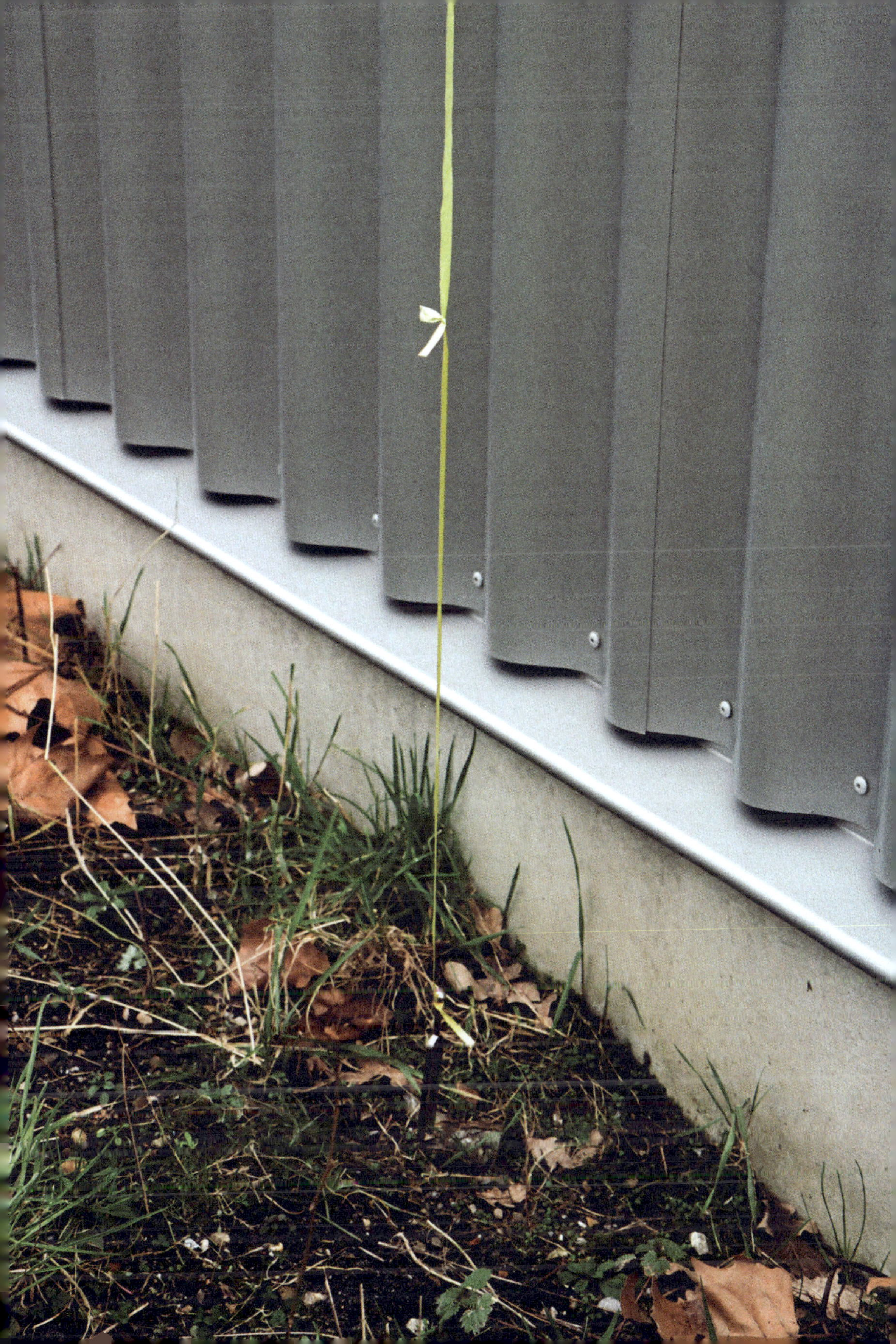

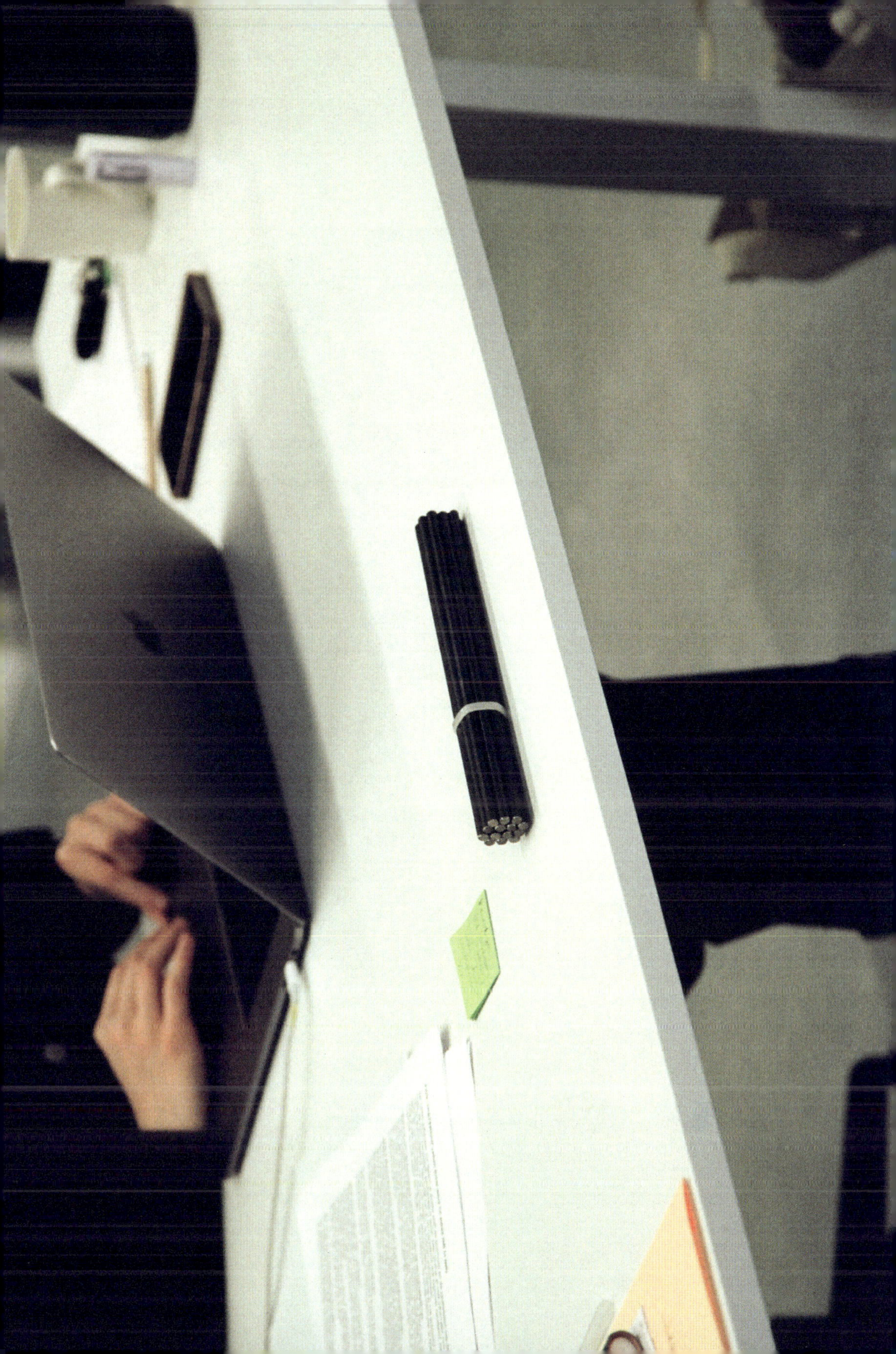

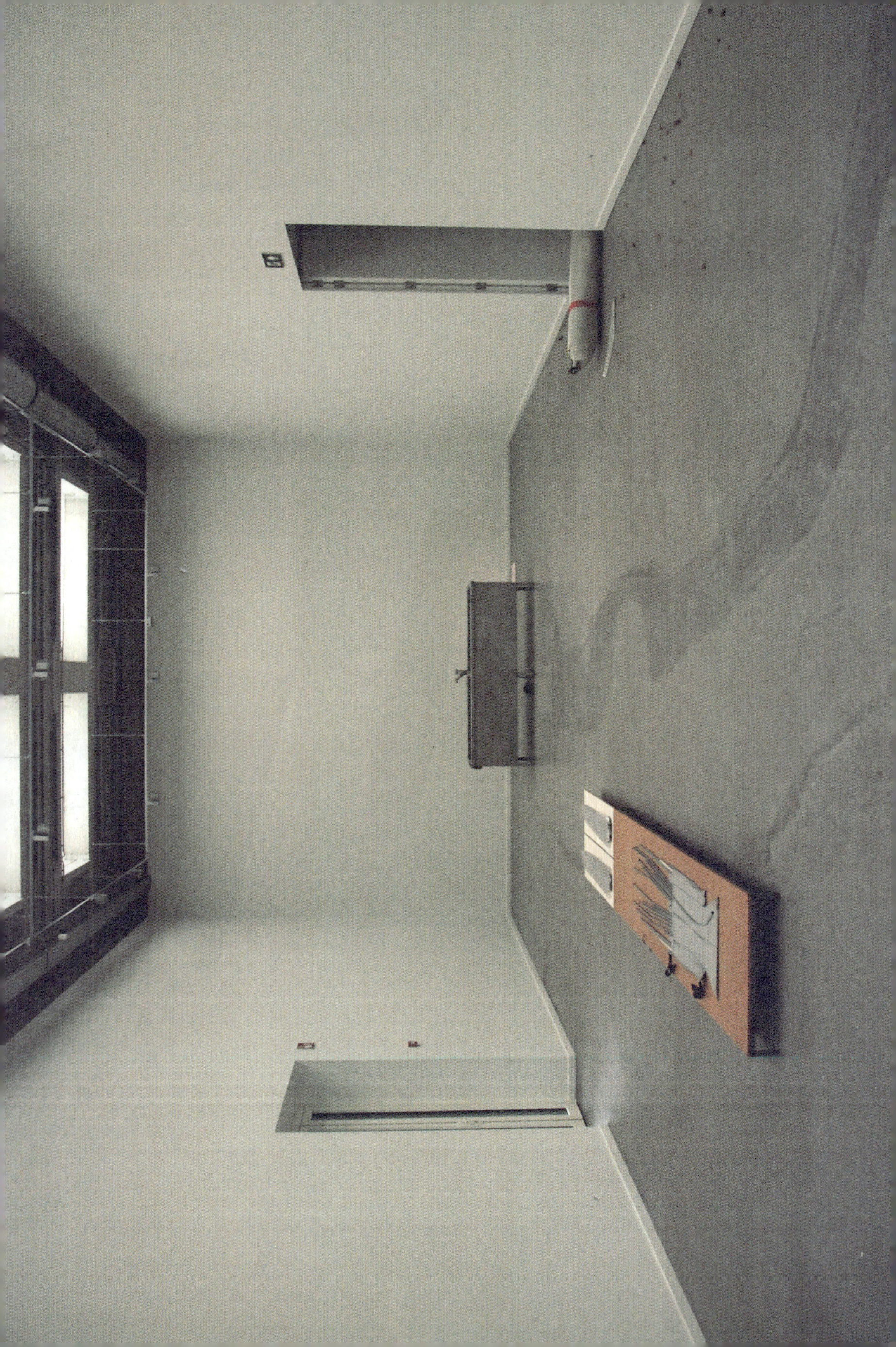

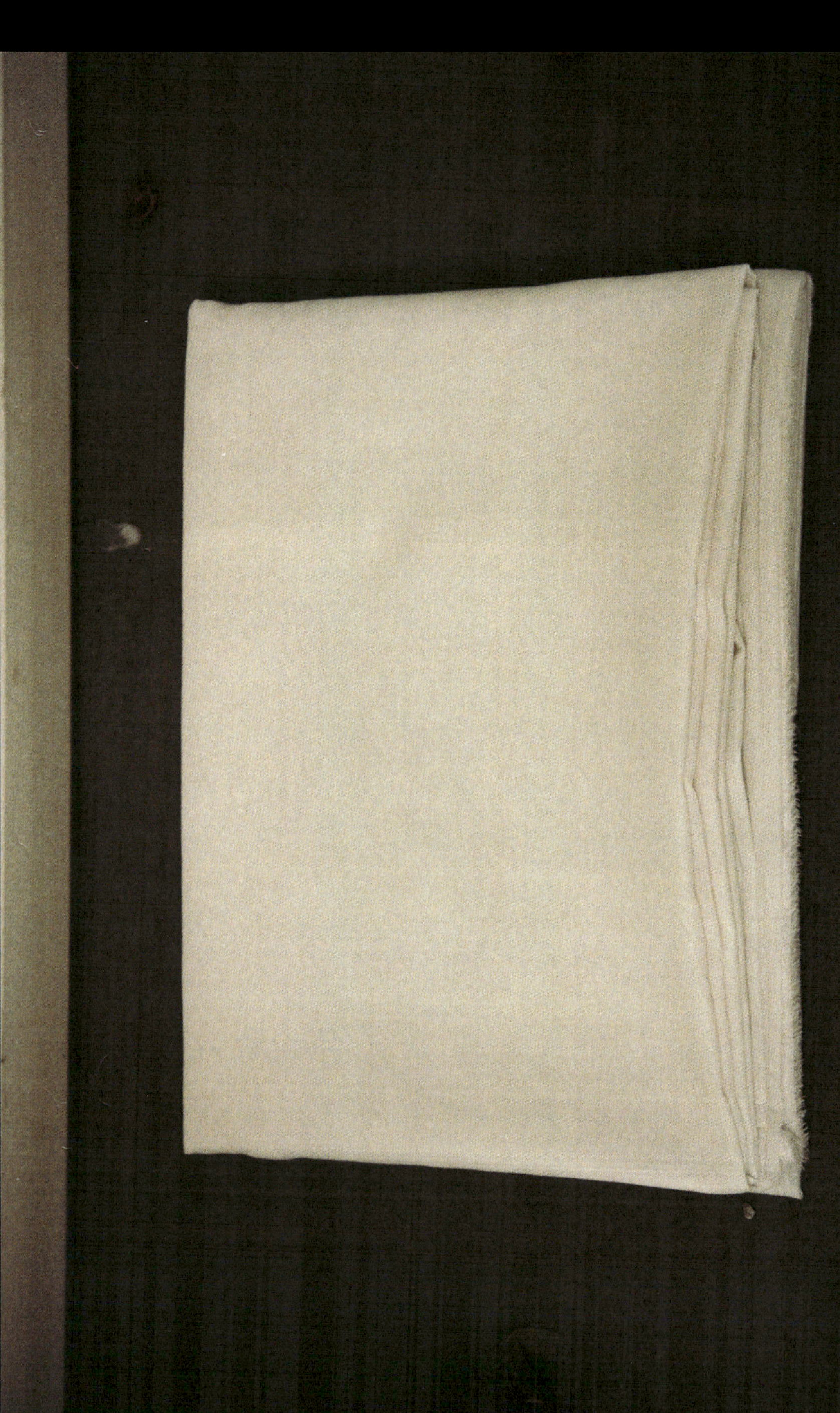

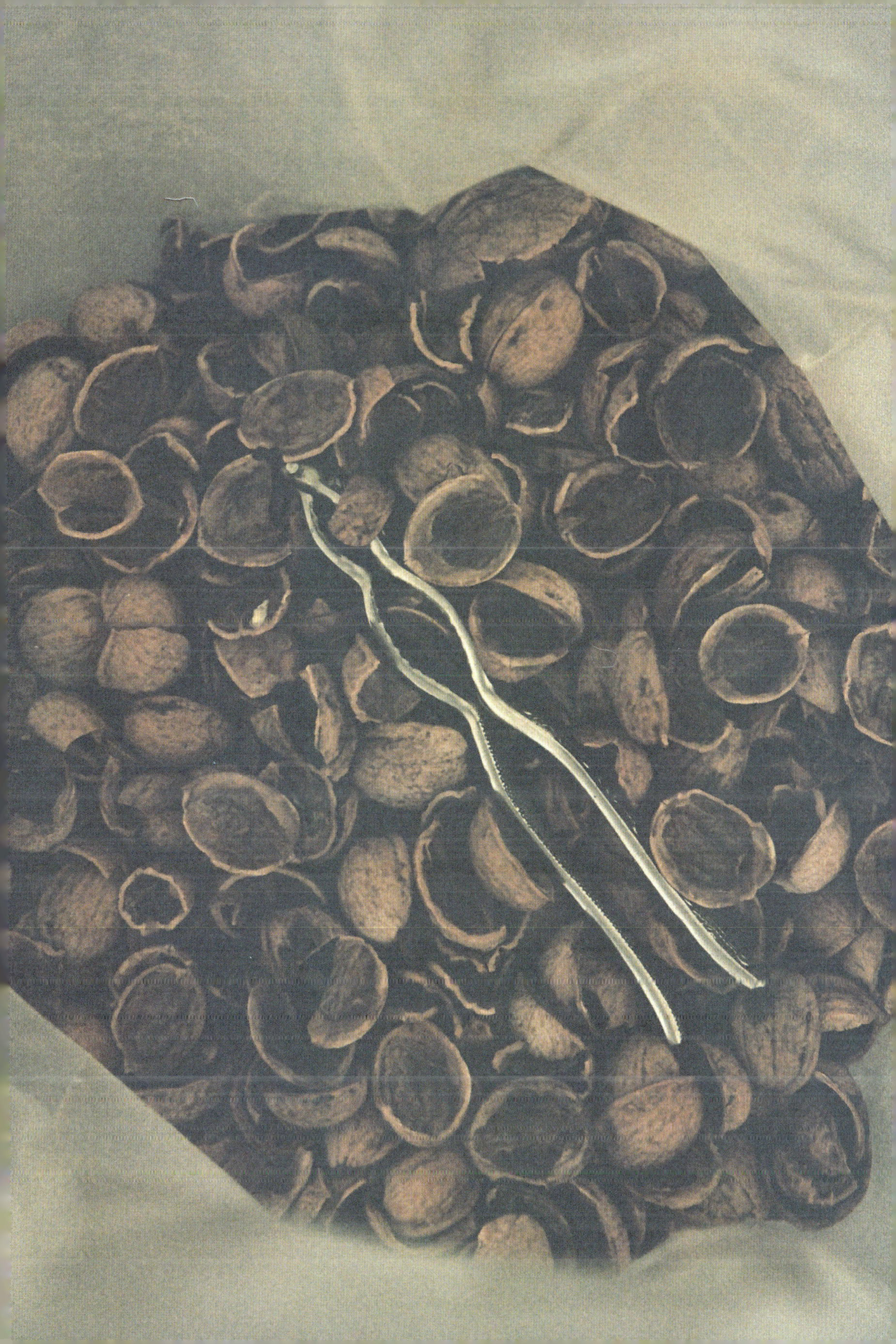

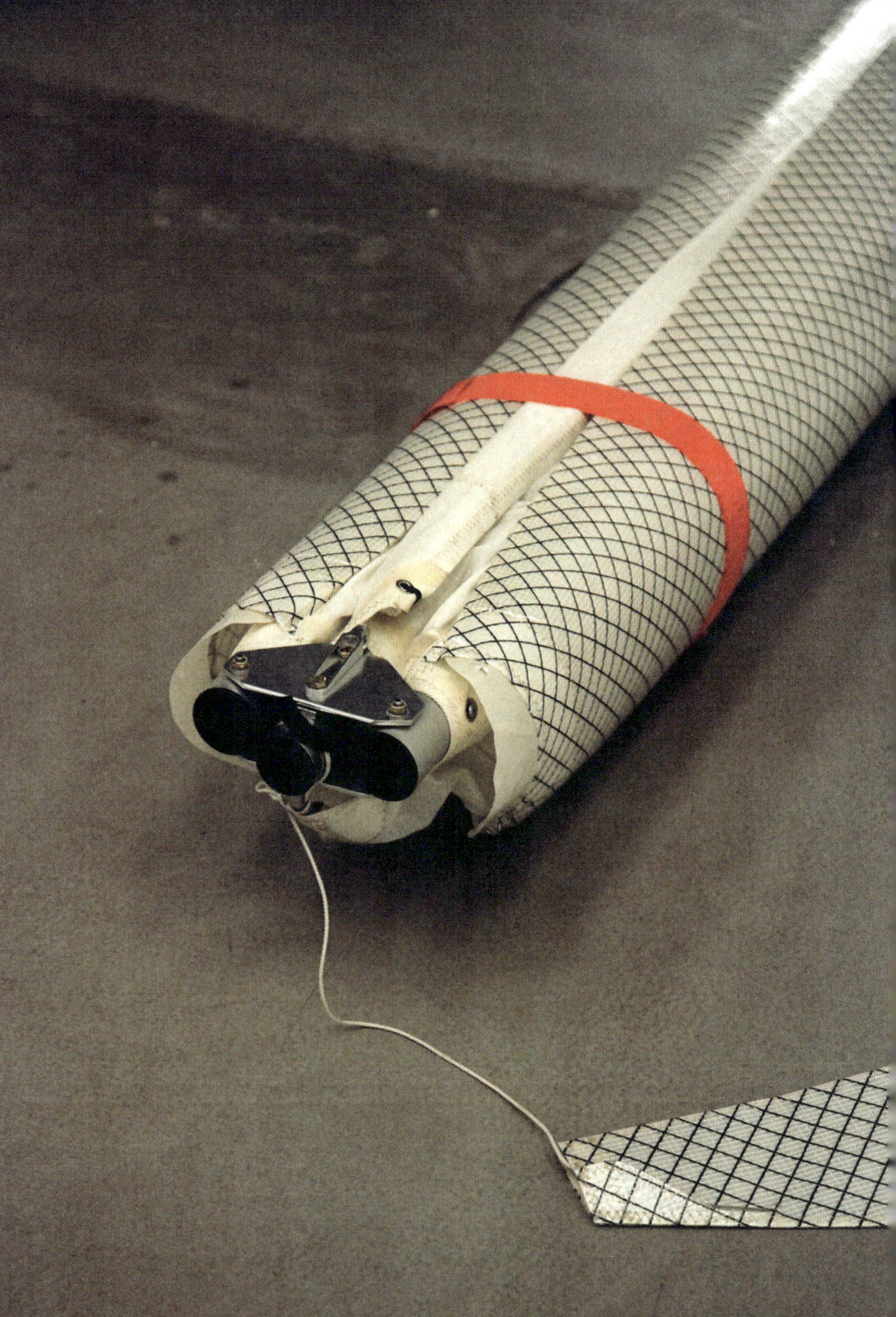

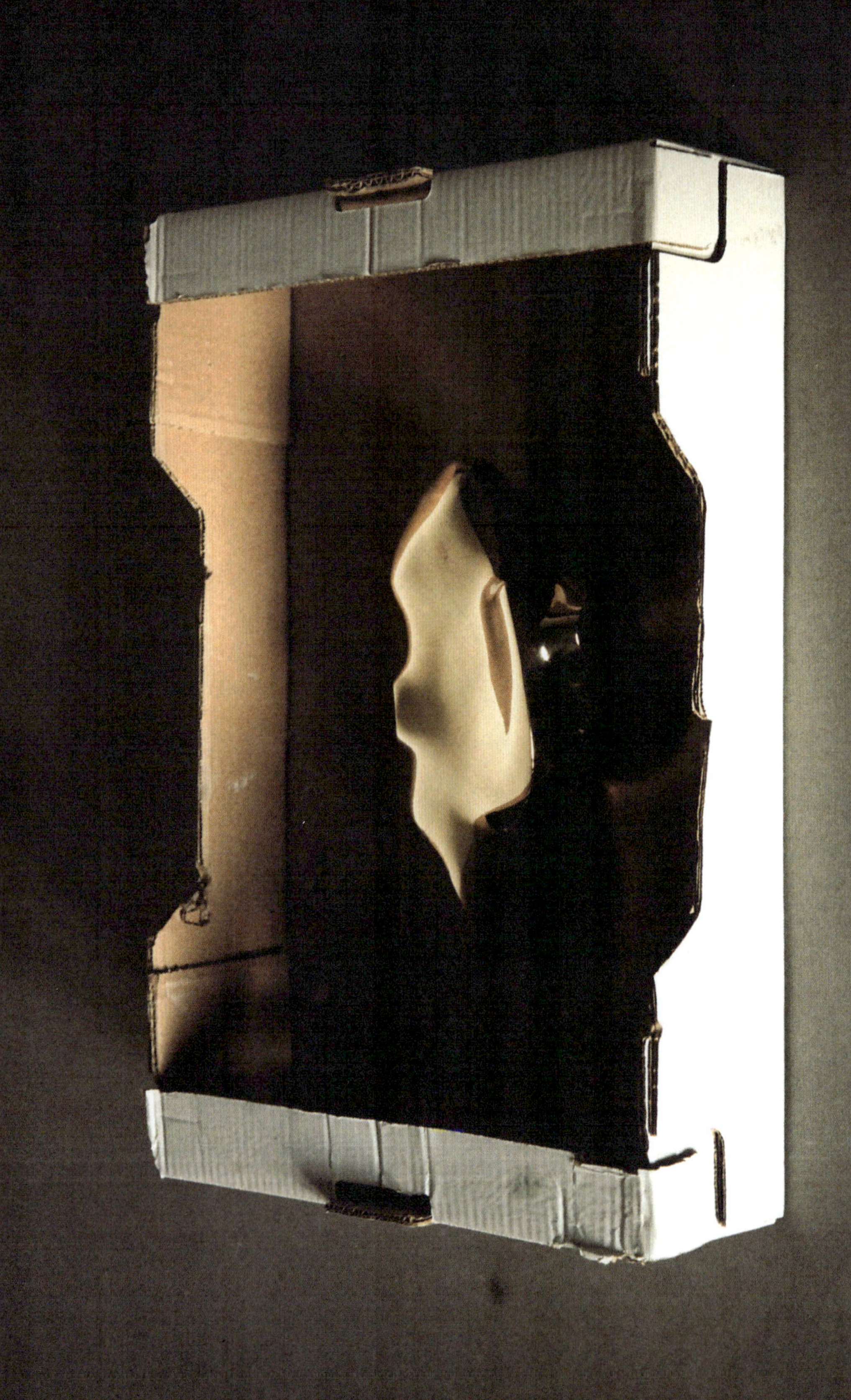

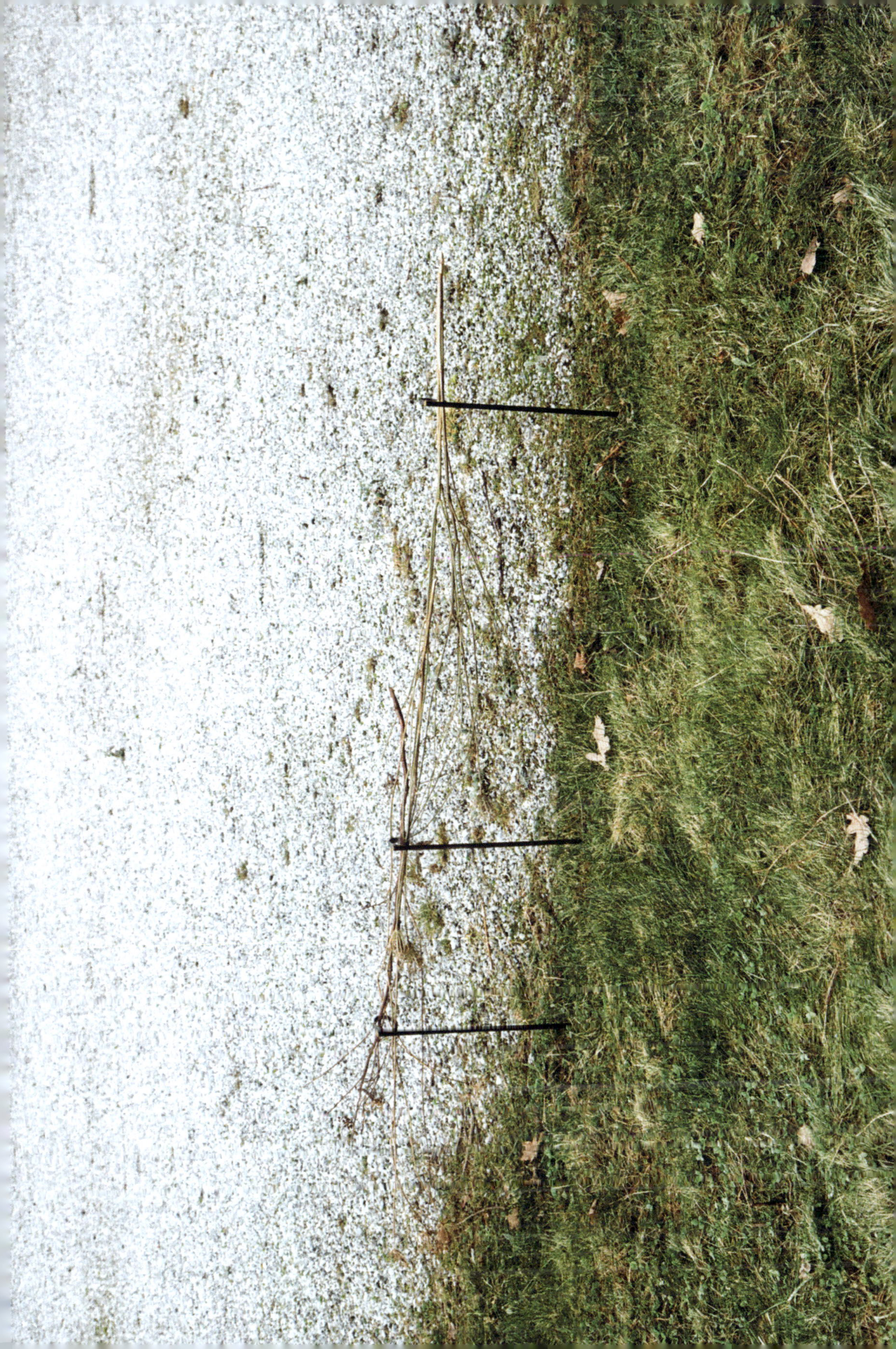

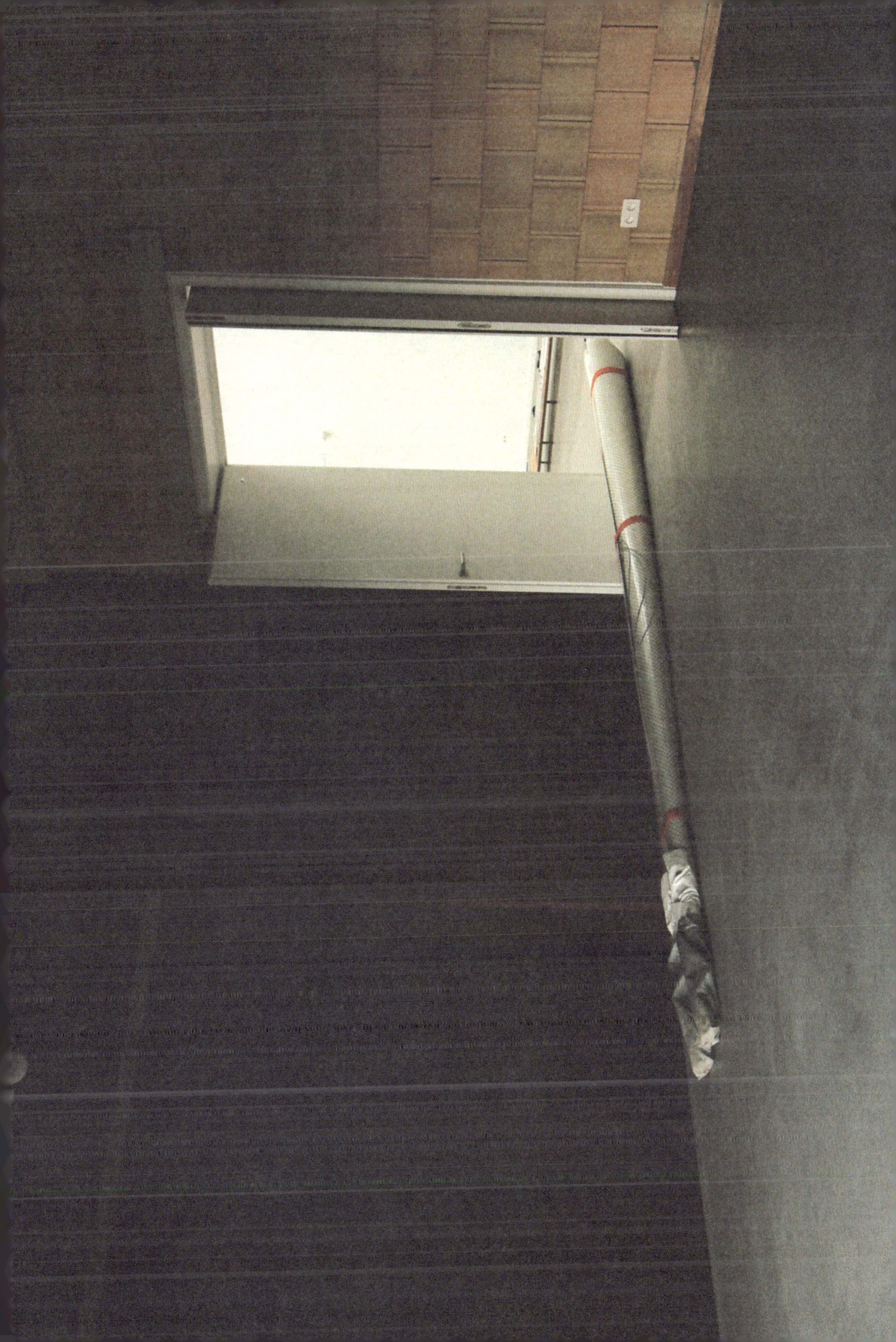

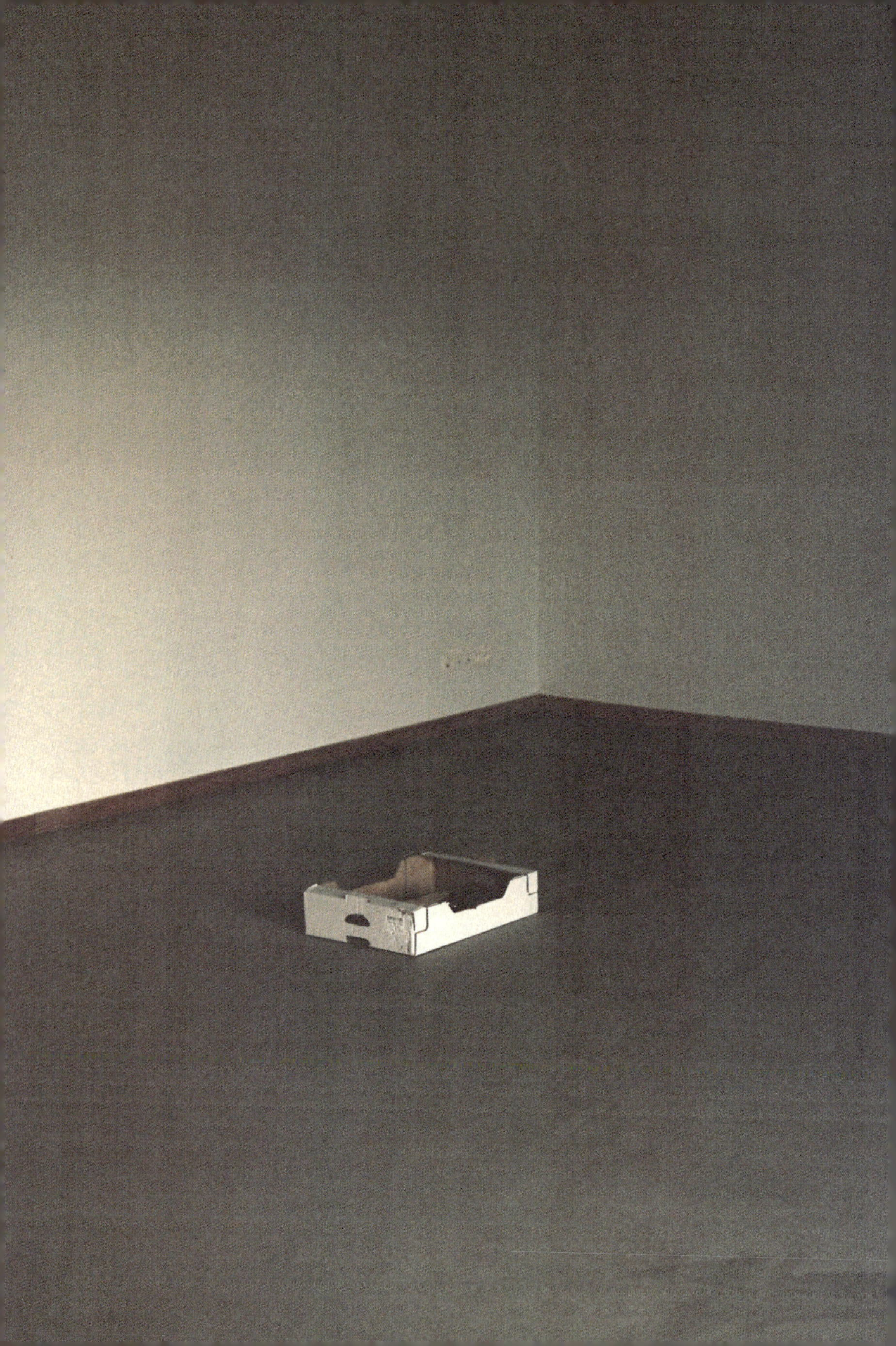

This publication is published on the occasion of the exhibition
*Fugue*
Aaron Amar Bhamra & Céline Mathieu

February 15 – May 11, 2025
Jester
Schachtboklaan 11,
3600 Genk, Belgium
jester.be

*General and Business Director*
Yesim Bektas

*Artistic Director*
Koi Persyn

*Assistant Curator*
Karel Op 't Eynde

*Production coordinator*
Stefanie De Bakker

*Production staff*
Stef Renard, Rachel Daniëls

*Administration officer*
Clara Tashjian


*Fugue* was produced in collaboration with Phileas – The Austrian
Office for Contemporary Art and with the support of the
Flemish Government, the City of Genk, the Federal Ministry
for Arts, Culture, Civil Service and Sport (BMKOES) of
Austria and the Austrian Cultural Forum Brussels.

*Acknowledgments*
Monika Georgieva, Hardev Bhamra, Andrea Bhamra, Naomi
Bhamra, Thomas Supper, Anna Pöll, Fridolin Welte, Angelika
Gassner, Joëlle Laederach, Ginevra Petrozzi, Andrea Zavala
Folache, Penélope Cleo de Zavala Jensen, Matt Hinkley, Gabriel
Pericàs, Elouan Le Bars, Luc Haenen, Max Parnell, Wauthier
de Mahieu, Rosie Broadhead, Kasper De Vos, Mathias MU,
Jan Omer Fack, Stef Renard, Tom Hallet, Travis Broussard,
Charlotte Fexer, celador's Yann Chateigné Tytelman and
Alicja Melzacka.

Catalogue
*Aaron Amar Bhamra & Céline Mathieu: Fugue*

*Edited by*
Aaron Amar Bhamra, Céline Mathieu, Koi Persyn

*Publishing Editor*
Emma Passarella, Mousse

*Graphic Design*
Anna Azzali, Mousse

*Contributions*
Aaron Amar Bhamra, Céline Mathieu, Koi Persyn,
Johanna Schindler, Eloise Sweetman, Charlie Usher

*Copyediting and Proofreading*
Afro Xylanthé

© 2025 Jester, Genk
© 2025 Mousse Publishing
© 2025 the artists, the authors for their texts

All works by Céline Mathieu: Courtesy of Gauli Zitter

*Photographic credits*
Aaron Amar Bhamra, Stef Renard,
vandenbussche-vandenbossche

*Published and distributed by*
Mousse Publishing
Contrappunto s.r.l.
via Pier Candido Decembrio, 28
20137, Milan–Italy
moussemagazine.it

*First edition*
2025

*Printed by*
Àncora Arti Grafiche, Italy

ISBN 978-88-6749-680-8

€ 20 / $ 25



*On the cover*
BACK: (8) Céline Mathieu, *Bekken*, 2025 (detail)
FRONT: (2) Aaron Amar Bhamra, *midair*, 2025 / *Kite (sleep-like)*,
2025 (detail)

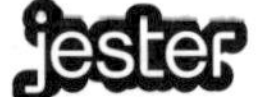 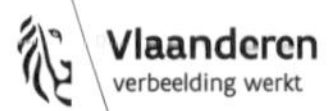 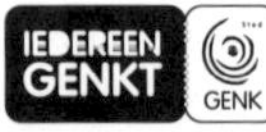 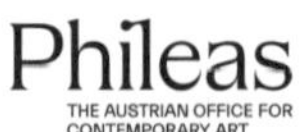